# AN INTRODUCTION TO ANGLO-WELSH LITERATURE

RAYMOND GARLICK

D1477746

UNIVERSITY OF WALES PRESS
on behalf of the
WELSH ARTS COUNCIL

First published *Writers of Wales* series 1970. This edition 1972.

© UNIVERSITY OF WALES PRESS 1972

ISBN 0 7083 0510 5

PRINTED IN
WALES BY
A. McLAY & CO., LTD.,
CARDIFF

# PROLOGUE

This essay, commissioned by the Welsh Arts Council for the Writers of Wales series, was first published by the University of Wales Press in 1970. That finely produced and limited edition was exhausted by the spring of 1972, and I am grateful to the editors of the series – Dr R. Brinley Jones and Mr Meic Stephens – for arranging for the publication of this new, ordinary edition.

The resetting of the text has made possible the rewriting of some . paragraphs and the inclusion of new material, though no major change has been made. The subject is continually growing, and at both ends. At the contemporary end, the past two years have seen the publication of a number of new books and records, and of poems and critical articles in the Anglo-Welsh periodicals. There have been some stimulating and well-attended short courses on Anglo-Welsh Literature, under the aegis of Yr Academi Gymreig and other bodies, and the Writers in Schools scheme has given a large number of young people a direct contact with some of the writers of Wales in the English language. New anthologies of Anglo-Welsh poetry for primary, middle and secondary schools are in preparation. At Trinity College, Carmarthen, the first course to feature Anglo-Welsh Literature as a full component in its own right has been established, and similar developments are occurring elsewhere. Radio and television have also paid some attention to the contemporary literature of Wales in English. It may nonetheless be thought that the most significant development is represented by a lecture to a Welsh summer school in 1970, by a Welsh critic, Mr Dafydd Elis Thomas, whose thesis was that contemporary Welsh and Anglo-Welsh poets speak with one mind.

Few of these points of growth are reflected in the revision of the text of this book. In relation to contemporary Anglo-Welsh Literature it is an Introduction in the sense of a preliminary. It is concerned mainly with the past that has led up to this present. About the present, information is easily obtainable – in THE ANGLO-WELSH REVIEW, POETRY WALES, PLANET, and MABON; in the Introductions to the two new anthologies TWENTY-FIVE WELSH SHORT STORIES and THE SHINING PYRAMID; in the monographs of the Writers of Wales series; and above all in Glyn Jones's THE DRAGON HAS TWO TONGUES.

About previous centuries so little information has been available as almost to justify the unlikely assumption that a past did not exist – were it not for two large improbabilities: that English should have been used in Wales for so long without giving rise to literary expression, and that the vigorous Anglo-Welsh Literature of the twentieth century should have sprung into existence fully formed. It was the function of this essay to begin to scrutinize those improbabilities.

Its juxtaposition of the writers of the past with those of the present has been questioned in an ingenious and delightful manner by the application to it of Fluellen's Macedon-Monmouth non-sequitur. But justly to represent the argument, Fluellen's words would have to be rewritten: 'There *is* a river at Monmouth, and there *was* a river at Monmouth . . . 'tis alike as my fingers is to my fingers, and there have been salmons in it for centuries'. It is to the river of their origin that the salmon return, and there alone they breed –

> *The echo of once being here*
> *Possesses and inclines them*

to quote John Ormond's fine poem;

> *They ache towards the one world*
> *From which their secret*
> *Sprang, perpetuate*
> *More than themselves, the ritual*
> *Claim of the river . . .*

There is a sense in which this book is about 'the ritual claim of the river'.

With the reviewer who suggested that the title of the book should really be AN INTRODUCTION TO ANGLO-WELSH POETRY the writer has some sympathy, having inadvertently referred to it as such himself. However, as the revised concluding paragraphs of section III propose, the strongest elements of the Anglo-Welsh tradition are to be seen in the poetry. On the other hand, a preliminary to more than the poetry was attempted – while accepting that the short-story and the novel are twentieth century Anglo-Welsh phenomena and thus, in the design of the Writers of Wales series, to be treated in the monographs on Caradoc Evans, Arthur Machen, Alun Lewis, and so forth.

Another reviewer has taken issue with the title on the ground that the book is not an Introduction to Anglo-Welsh Literature but an Introduction to Anglo-Welsh literary antecedents. I cannot myself think of Swrdwal or George Herbert, Morgan Llwyd or Henry Vaughan, under the discouraging nomenclature of 'an Anglo-Welsh literary antecedent'. They were writers, and Anglo-Welsh writers, in exactly the same sense as twentieth century ones are – which, of course, is perfectly compatible with being, from another point of view, in the mainstream of English Literature at the same time.

The obvious justification for a concern with the past of Anglo-Welsh Literature is that it exists, that it has a certain literary interest in its own right, and that it sheds some light on the present. But during the past year the social and educational implications touched upon towards the end of section XVIII have increased in significance. As never before, language has emerged as a major concern. It is not the Welsh language that is the problem. The problem there, as with colour or Catholicism elsewhere, is not a problem of language – or race, or religion – but one of justice, of civil and human rights. Naturally, all who are sensitive to language – any language (English, for example), language as a phenomenon, as a human mystery, as a profound statement of individuality – have reacted to these assaults upon civil rights in matters of language with righteous anger. The letter from four Anglo-Welsh writers published in THE TIMES of 28th May 1971 articulated the appalled censure of this injustice by many English-speakers.

The Welsh language itself is in no sense a problem because its right to be in Wales, its relationship to the life of Wales, its function here, are self-evident. The problem language in Wales is English. How did it get here? How long has it been here? What is its role here? Can it be justified here? How should it be taught here? What should be its status here in relation to Welsh? These are profound questions, much too important to be left to judges, lord chancellors, secretaries of State, naive amateurs in such matters. These are questions for the guardians and professionals of the language – the Anglo-Welsh writers first of all, and after them the teachers.

The long history of English as a language of Wales, of its complementary relationship to Welsh, of its use by writers of Wales down the centuries as an instrument of beauty and precision, must make it unbearable that it should ever be employed as a crude political counter, as an instrument of injustice, as a bludgeoning or provincializing or alienating force. If this essay has any contemporary relevance, its writer would wish that it might lie in some contribution to concerned thought about these questions.

Raymond Garlick
*Trinity College Carmarthen*
*May 1972*

# I

The term Anglo-Welsh was perhaps coined by Evan Evans (1731–1788)—who, since most of his writing was in the Welsh language, is better known by his bardic name of Ieuan Brydydd Hir. What he refers to as his "first performance in the English tongue"—a long poem entitled THE LOVE OF OUR COUNTRY— was published in 1772 at Carmarthen. It is prefaced by a two-page address to the reader, in which the epithet Anglo-Welsh appears— though applied not to poets but to prelates. The term thus originates (if this is its first appearance) as a sign of contradiction, and in its later, literary application this element is still discernible. As recently as 1969 the editors of THE LILTING HOUSE, the first comprehensive anthology of twentieth century Anglo-Welsh poetry, were obliged to regret the omission of "one poet . . . who takes such strong objection to the term Anglo-Welsh that he will not allow any of his work to be published under this heading".

In the literary context to which the term has now become limited, this contradiction—the compounded ascription of Englishness and Welshness—is apparent rather than real. It is convenient shorthand for "writing in the English language by Welshmen": a linguistic distinction, implying no reflection upon the Welshness of the writers in question. It is in fact a termino-logical exactitude—the embodiment in a convenient epithet (since reference to Anglo-Welsh Literature implies that there exists something else to which the term Welsh Literature is properly reserved) of the bilingual nature of literary activity in Wales.

Other terms have been used. Earlier anthologies of original poetry or prose in the English language by Welsh writers have been content to describe the writing as Welsh: thus MODERN WELSH POETRY, WELSH SHORT STORIES. More exactly, two anthologies— WELSH POETS (1917) and WELSH VOICES (1967)—have applied the epithet Welsh to the writers rather than the writing. It is perhaps significant that all these books were published in London. Objections to the appropriation of the term Welsh by publications whose contents were entirely in the English language crystallized in comment by some critics in Wales at the time of the appearance of Keidrych Rhys's anthology MODERN WELSH POETRY (1944), though in 1938 Mr Saunders Lewis had noted that "with rare exceptions English literary critics have never heard that there was, or is, a Welsh literature in a Welsh language, so that when they discuss writers such as Edward Thomas or W. H. Davies they do not call them Anglo-Welsh writers but simply Welsh". The 1944 anthology was an important collection, but it was pointed out that its title was misleading—some found it offensive —in that the book did not contain one poem in Welsh. Such criticism articulated the view that to attach to writing in the English language the epithet Welsh was at best ambiguous, and— given the circumstance that many people outside Wales were un- aware that even the Welsh language existed—gratuitously perpet- uated ignorance of the existence of a living literature in Welsh.

By the nineteen sixties the force of this objection appears to have been felt: THE OXFORD BOOK OF WELSH VERSE (1962) and THE PENGUIN BOOK OF WELSH VERSE (1967) are both concerned with the older literature of Wales, the former in the original language and the latter in translation. Conversely, the two most significant English-language anthologies to appear in the 'sixties—THIS WORLD OF WALES (1968) and THE LILTING HOUSE (1969)—are both sub-titled "An Anthology of Anglo-Welsh Poetry", and published from Wales (the last in association with a London publisher). If the epithet Anglo-Welsh is still, for some, a sign of contradiction, most of the writers it now describes would prob- ably prefer to bear with such ambiguity rather than that the status of literature in Welsh should in any way be misconceived.

Preoccupation with a literary terminology for writing in the English language by Welshmen (and thus with the nature of the phenomena which it was intended to define) seems to have begun in the twenties of the present century. The curiously exacerbating epithet Cymric, for writing in the Welsh language, was given a certain currency, and the hybrid Anglo-Cymric briefly flowered. At this time, too, we find Mr Saunders Lewis thinking within the concept of an Anglo-Celtic literature—a composite literature in English of the Celtic peoples of the British Isles. "There have been writers of English who were of Welsh blood or Manx or Scottish," he observes, but "Anglo-Celtic literature is almost entirely an Irish product. The other Celtic races have added very little to it."

Nonetheless the more precise and obvious compound was to suggest itself, and in the correspondence columns of the August 1922 number of THE WELSH OUTLOOK—the periodical in which much of this discussion was taking place—there appears a letter headed "Anglo-Welsh Poetry". The writer is H. Idris Bell, and in his letter he refers to "the poets of what I may call the Anglo-Welsh movement"; he goes on to suggest that "there may hereafter arise a poet to do for Anglo-Welsh literature what W. B. Yeats has done for Anglo-Irish". It is perhaps appropriate that the term and concept Anglo-Welsh, in its literary application, should have been launched upon its course in the twentieth century by an Englishman devoted to Wales, to Welsh Literature, and to the attempt to convey something of its life through translation into English. If Sir Idris Bell is best remembered for his translation of Dr Thomas Parry's HISTORY OF WELSH LITERATURE, the other literature of Wales also has cause to honour his memory.

Assisted perhaps by the model of Anglo-Irish, the new term gained gradual acceptance. It appears, in quotation marks, in the second number of Keidrych Rhys's magazine WALES (August 1937)—"This review ought to be a sort of forum where the 'Anglo-Welsh' have their say"—and is used (without quotation marks) in Wyn Griffith's review of the first number in THE TIMES LITERARY SUPPLEMENT. In December 1938 Mr Saunders Lewis employs it in the interrogative title of a lecture delivered to the Cardiff branch of the Guild of Graduates of the University of Wales: IS THERE AN ANGLO-WELSH LITERATURE?

By the nineteen fifties the usage was widespread. In 1955 THE TIMES LITERARY SUPPLEMENT opened a full-length article entitled "The Two Literatures of Wales" with a firm indicative: "There are now in Wales two literatures, Welsh and Anglo-Welsh", and in the ensuing year an article of similar proportions was headed "Anglo-Welsh Attitudes". In 1957 the University of Wales Press gave its august imprimatur to the term—in the printed form of a memorial lecture given by one of the most distinguished of Anglo-Welsh writers, Gwyn Jones, in his capacity as Rendel Professor of English Language and Literature at University College, Aberystwyth. The lecture, THE FIRST FORTY YEARS, was sub-titled "Some notes on Anglo-Welsh Literature". In recognition of this general acceptance of the term, the only English-language literary review then in publication in Wales, in its summer 1958 number, in the ninth year of its appearance, changed its title from DOCK LEAVES to THE ANGLO-WELSH REVIEW—under which title it has appeared ever since.

There remains to be considered one further term which has frequently been used as an alternative to Anglo-Welsh. By the imperfectly informed and less discriminating, Anglo-Welsh writers and their works are habitually described as English. Linguistically, of course, this is perfectly proper, and as a linguistic distinction it was the usage of earlier Anglo-Welsh poets. "What have I," said Evan Evans in the address to the reader prefaced to his 1772 poem THE LOVE OF OUR COUNTRY, "what have I, who am a Welshman, to do with English Poetry?" His answer is that his intention is interpretative as well as reciprocal: "I have done it in English verse in order that men of learning in both languages may understand it". In point of fact the poem is primarily addressed to the reader over the border—it is essentially a poem that sets out to interpret Wales to the outsider. Moreover, he was writing from a Wales that was largely Welsh-speaking. By calling it an English poem he means precisely a poem in the English language.

When, however, the contemporary Anglo-Welsh writer finds

himself described—particularly in a London publication—as an English poet, he is likely to find the epithet ambiguous. Does the fact that a man writes in the English language make him English, and a contributor to English Literature? "Despite our speech we are not English": most Anglo-Welsh writers would endorse R. S. Thomas's line. As to contributing to English Literature, in the sense of the literature of England, it is clear that much Anglo-Welsh writing articulates (in Yeats's phrase) "a separate world from that of England". No Englishman would accept for a moment that R. S. Thomas's poetry, for example, or Emyr Humphreys' novels, are about the world of England.

In the twenties and thirties of the present century the great achievements of Anglo-Irish Literature made it an influential model of a literature in English but not of England. However, as early as 1894 other models had been proposed for the Anglo-Welsh situation. In a remarkable editorial prefaced to the first number of his magazine WALES, published in that year, Sir Owen M. Edwards wrote: "There is, undoubtedly, something like a literary awakening among English-speaking Welshmen; there is a strong desire for a literature that will be English in language but Welsh in spirit . . . . Why should the land of Henry Vaughan and George Herbert be less fond of literature than the land of Islwyn and Ceiriog? . . . Why should not the English literature of Wales have characteristics of its own—like Scotch literature and American literature?"

In recent years the distinction between English Literature—the literature of England—and a whole series of national literatures in the English language has been clearly made. Volumes of Scottish, American, Canadian, South African, Australian, New Zealand, poetry are readily available. Second national literatures in English are emerging from a number of new African countries. It is in such a context that Anglo-Welsh Literature finds its identity.

Where in terms of chronological origin does Anglo-Welsh Literature take its place in this series? In Ireland the beginnings of a national literature in English are first made possible towards the middle of the seventeenth century. Ann Bradstreet, who is generally taken as the first American poet, was born (in England) about 1612 and her first collection of poems was published in 1650. Canadian Literature in English began in Nova Scotia in the second half of the eighteenth century. In the antipodes, FIRST FRUITS OF AUSTRALIAN POETRY was published in 1819. The origins of Anglo-Welsh poetry appear to antedate all these.

# II

An empirical approach to the origins and dating of Anglo-Welsh
Literature (as distinct from interesting but arbitrary personal
theories on the subject) seems to involve the answering of two or
three questions. First, the linguistic one: how far back can we
observe English being used as a language of Wales? Second, having established this, do we observe thereafter any undoubted
Welshmen using the English language for literary purposes? If so,
what is their writing to be called but Anglo-Welsh Literature?

The history of English as a language of Wales perhaps begins with
Asser, monk of St. David's, who about 885 agreed to spend part of
each year in the service of Alfred of Wessex, and the other part in
Wales. He was obviously literate in Old English. Again, in the
first decade of the twelfth century Henry I of England established
a colony of Flemings in south Pembrokeshire: they appear to
have abandoned their own language and taken to English, so that
that region of Wales has been English-speaking for some
eight centuries.

To pass from the individual and the local to more widespread
tendencies, in 1284 the Statute of Rhuddlan brought much of
Wales under the rule of the English king, and the crown officers
and garrisons of the new castles and boroughs eventually created
English-speaking pockets within the country, which gradually
spread up the principal valleys. THE HUGHES PARRY REPORT ON THE
LEGAL STATUS OF THE WELSH LANGUAGE, that interesting but almost
wholly unimplemented blueprint for justice, observes that "There
emerged in Wales during the Middle Ages a class of professional
lawyers and clerks who were proficient in Welsh, English, French
and Latin . . . Nearly all legal and quasi-legal documents, such as
deeds, wills, manorial or borough records, surviving from
medieval Wales are in Latin or in English". Professor Glanmor
Williams has drawn attention to another aspect of life in medieval

Wales which made for a certain knowledge of English, namely the considerable amount of movement—much more than is often supposed—which took place between the two countries: "Drovers took their cattle to English markets, weavers their cloth. Every harvest-season gangs of Welsh reapers made their way to English counties to work for a few weeks". Moreover Welsh mercenaries and merchants, pilgrims and students, acquired some English on their travels.

One such was the author of the HYMN TO THE VIRGIN, written about 1470: it seems likely that his name was Ieuan ap Hywel Swrdwal. A Welsh student at Oxford, he wrote his poem as a challenge to his English contemporaries there. In answer to their baiting he announced that he would compose a poem in English such as all the Englishmen in England could not compose. A glance at the resulting composition shows why: the language is English, the spelling is Welsh, and the poem employs four patterns of alliteration and internal rhyme (*cynghanedd*). Here are stanzas 4 and 5:

> *Wi sin ddy bricht kwin wyth kwning/ and blys,*
> *ddy bloswm ffruwt bering;*
> *ei wowld, as owld as ei sing,*
> *wynn iwr lwf on iwr lofing.*

> *Kwin od off owr God, owr geiding/ mwdyr,*
> *maedyn notwythstanding,*
> *hwo wed syts wyth a ryts ring*
> *as God wod ddys gwd weding.*

In the English of five hundred years later they might be literally rendered as follows:

> *We see the bright queen with wisdom/ and bliss,*
> *the blossom bearing fruit;*
> *I would, as long as I sing,*
> *win your love in praising you.*

*Sole queen of our God, our guiding/ mother,*
*maiden notwithstanding,*
*who wed such with a rich ring,*
*since God desired this good wedding.*

Since the Welsh orthography of the original records English pronunciation before 1500 as it sounded to a Welshman, the poem is of considerable linguistic interest. However, it is not without literary significance—particularly in its technique.

The poem is an address to Christ—first through his mother, and afterwards directly—in which the poet prays that he may lead a good life, die a good death, and thereafter see amid "north and noon/ and sun and moon/ the Son in might". With its images of branch and tree, blossom and fruit, of queen, king and crown, it has something of the freshness and naivety of many medieval lyrics on the same theme, but a vigour and tightness of texture which are all its own. There are 96 lines, arranged in thirteen stanzas: the first seven are quatrains and the remaining six are more intricate structures of twelve lines each.

The quatrains contain thirty syllables each, distributed in lines of 10, 6, 7 and 7 syllables. One end-rhyme is used throughout each stanza, but in the first line of every quatrain this occurs in the eighth syllable (once in the seventh). In the concluding couplet of each quatrain, one of the lines has a masculine and the other a feminine ending. The four lines thus form the shaft, the short line and the two wings of an *englyn*.

The succeeding long stanzas (two of them have lines lacking) are constructed of four octosyllabic lines plus eight lines of four syllables each: the rhyme scheme is ababcccbcccb. Here is the concluding stanza:

*Owr lwk, owr king, owr lok, owr kae—*
*mei God, ei prae, mei geid wpricht!*
*Ei sik, ei sing, ei siak, ei sae,*

*ei wer awae, a wiri wicht.*
*Agast ei go,*
*mei ffrynds mi ffro.*
*Ei ffond a ffo,*
*wy ffynd ei fficht;*
*eil sing awlso*
*yn welth an wo*
*(ei kann no mo)*
*tw kwin o micht.*

And a modern literal version:

*Our luck, our king, our lock, our key—*
*my God, I pray, my upright guide!*
*I seek, I sing, I shake, I say,*
*I wear away, a weary wight.*
*Aghast I go,*
*deserted by my friends.*
*I find a foe,*
*with fiend I fight;*
*I'll sing also*
*in wealth and woe*
*(I can do no more)*
*to the queen of might.*

The tight texture is achieved not merely by the repetition of
syllabic and rhyme schemes throughout the two stanza systems
of which the poem is composed, but by an internal binding of the
lines through alliteration and internal rhyme in one or other of four
patterns. There are lines in which a syllable in the first half rhymes
with the penultimate syllable of a feminine ending (*cynghanedd
lusg*):

as hi mae *tak/* ws w*ak*ing (line 27)

There are lines in which each consonant in the first half is repeated
in the same order in the second half, while in the middle there is

an unrelated element (*cynghanedd draws*):

tw *hefn ffwl*/ wel/ tw *haf* on *fflcht* (line 32)

There are lines in which the alliterations of the first and second halves of the line correspond exactly, without the intervention of an unrelated part (*cynghanedd groes*):

*Michti*, i *twk*,/ *mi* o*cht* *tw* tel (line 29)

Finally, there are lines which fall into three parts, and in which the last syllable of the first part rhymes with the last of the second, while the second alliterates with the third (*cynghanedd sain*):

Kwin *od*/ off owr *God*,/ owr *geiding* (line 17)

The author of the HYMN TO THE VIRGIN is (to quote one of his own lines) "a gwd, mit wricht"—a good, proper workman. The assumptions that control the handling of language in this early Anglo-Welsh poem, and in many that succeed it, derive from the bardic tradition of poetry in the Welsh language. These assumptions are perhaps best illuminated by a comment in Dr. Thomas Parry's HISTORY OF WELSH LITERATURE, where attention is drawn to "the critical standpoint which determined Welsh poetry down to the end of the eighteenth century, that is to say, so long as the least element remained of what can properly be called the Welsh tradition. That standpoint is that sound is as important as sense; that metre and *cynghanedd*, the whole framework of verse, are as much a part of the aesthetic effect as what is said." Dr. Parry goes on to point out that "The tendency of modern criticism has been to consider primarily the thought expressed in a poem; as for the rhythm, the rhymes, the alliteration, they are desirable no doubt but are regarded as an adornment of the verse, additional elements, so to say, introduced to give beauty to the work. The poetry of today is read with the eye, and the eye is the door of the understanding. The poetry of old was heard with the ear, was recited or sung, and the ear is the gateway to the heart. The complex effect produced by the sound of answering consonants, rhymes floating on the hearing, old words bringing with them a fragment of the past into the memory and uniting yesterday and today . . . that was the way in which poetry gave satisfaction to our fathers."

Though preoccupation with wrought language is to be a mark of Anglo-Welsh poetry down the ages, the sheer technique of the HYMN TO THE VIRGIN is a *tour de force* to which perhaps the VISION AND PRAYER of Dylan Thomas, itself a religious poem of great intensity, is the best modern parallel.

# III

Not long after the probable date of composition of the Hymn
to the Virgin, Henry Tudor in 1485 succeeded to the English
throne—an event which promoted, among other changes in the
life of Wales, that process of bilingualism which was to be
hastened on its way by two of his successors, so that in a comparatively short time a whole class of Welshmen acquired the English
language.

In his poem At Bosworth A. G. Prys-Jones evokes that plain
in the English Midlands where these processes had their beginning:

*Cry "Tudor" here and these green fields will swarm*
*With companies of ghostly fighting men*
*Who marched from Wales to make a kinsman king.*

Having done so, they rode with him into London under the red
dragon of Cadwaladr, obtained posts at court, were enlisted in
the new bodyguard of the Yeoman of the Guard, flourished in
many trades, and in the courts of law. All this clearly had far-
reaching results in terms of language, both in London and at
home. Thus in 1521 a Welsh lawyer, William Owen of Henllys
in Pembrokeshire, published his Abridgement of the Common
Law—the first book by a Welshman to be printed. Welsh monks
in religious houses in England were also writing prose in the
English language. John Gwynedd (c. 1490–1562), monk of St.
Albans, born at Castellmarch in Llŷn, published his Confutacyon
of the First Part of Frith's Book in 1528. The Dictionary of
National Biography gives sixteen publications by Richard
Whitford (d. 1542) of Whitford in Flintshire, monk of Syon
House and friend of Erasmus and More. Professor Glanmor
Williams describes him as "A writer of English of no mean
talent".

Among those who moved across the border at this time was a branch of the princely Powys family—which returned to Wales in 1934 with the deliberate ascent to origins of John Cowper Powys, who settled first in Corwen and then in Blaenau Ffestiniog. He brought with him, on his mother's side, the blood of Donne—whose forefathers had also left Wales by the sixteenth century (as dean of St Paul's John Donne bore the arms of the Dwns of Kidwelly). Another family which crossed the border at this time was that of the novelist Richard Hughes, who records his own return as a deliberate resumption of roots.

This understandable tendency to bilingualism among more Welshmen, which was one of the consequences of the accession of Henry VII of England, hardened in the hands of his son and successor to an English-language policy for those who would flourish under the new dispensation. The Act of Union of 1536 explicitly provided that the language of the courts should be English: "All Justices . . . and all other officers and ministers of the lawe shall proclayme and kepe the sessions . . . and all other courtes . . . in the Englisshe Tonge . . . and all othes . . . affidavithes verdictes and wagers of lawe to be given . . . in the Englisshe Tonge". It was also laid down that only Welshmen who had a knowledge of English should hold any office in Wales: "From hensforth no personne or personnes that use the Welsshe speche or langage shall have or enjoy any manner office or fees within the Realme of Englonde Wales or other the Kinges dominions . . . onles he or they use and exercise the speche or langage of Englisshe". (The so-called "language clause" of the Act of 1536 was repealed by the Welsh Courts Act 1942.)

A contemporary Anglo-Welsh poet, John Tripp, has a poem on this event—entitled HENRY VIII, OF IGNOBLE MEMORY:
> "In the wick of my heart," he dribbled,
>   "I have all love and zeal and honour
>   for these people." Then he picked up a quill
>   and signed the lethal bond,

*stitching Wales into the cloth*
*of his realm, before retiring to bed*
*with his queen of the year.*

The consequences of this statute mark the second stage in the adoption of the English language by numbers of Welshmen. Those affected were not tradesmen but gentry and lawyers, and from them an interest in the literary use of English might be expected.

The changes in religion, the dissolution of the monasteries—some of which had been havens of Welsh learning, and the substitution of English for Latin as the language of worship (which has happened again in our own time), represent a third force in the dissemination of English. In 1563 an act was introduced into Parliament providing, among other things, that a copy of the Bible and the Book of Common Prayer in English were to be placed in each church together with the Welsh versions, so that those reading them might "by conferring both tongues together the sooner attain to the knowledge of the English tongue". These were policies which affected the parish clergy, and through them their congregations.

An illustration of this is perhaps to be seen in the Tir Iarll group of poets, who wrote in Glamorgan throughout the Tudor period. One of them, Tomas ab Ifan ap Rhys, inserts four lines of English (in Welsh orthography) into a thirty-four line poem in Welsh. Another is Sir Richard the Blackbird—Richard Wiliam, priest of a parish in east Glamorgan, who flourished between 1590 and 1630. He wrote in both languages, and one of his English poems is entitled SIR RICHARD'S CONFESSION. It is a poem of twenty-four octosyllabic lines, and in its structure it echoes some of the Welsh poems of this nest of writers. The lines consist of two parts, the last syllable of the first half rhyming with the last syllable of the second half. Here are the opening lines:

*j haf latly, bing tw bysy*
*jn law maters, lost my fethers*
*and haf bing dwl, jn my yowthffwl*
*daes and livyd, disgontentyd*
*my tym j spent, off profferment*
*most ungodly, and karlesly*
*that j dar not, hard hys my lot*
*tak my ffry wyl, withowt peryl.*

Closely connected with the religious changes was a fourth agency which worked for the promotion of the use of the English language: the new education. With the dissolution of the monasteries, the Welsh monastic schools had also disappeared. Instead there were established the new Tudor grammar schools, such as those at Abergavenny, Brecon, Bangor, Carmarthen, Cowbridge, and Ruthin, where the Welsh language had no place. At the same time it must be remembered that, even under the old order, the great-grandfather of Sir John Wynn (1553–1626)—himself a contributor to Anglo-Welsh prose with his HISTORY OF THE GWYDIR FAMILY— had been sent to school at Caernarfon "where he learnt the English tongue".

The tendency of the new grammar schools was completed by the first Protestant foundation at Oxford—that of Jesus College in 1571, which soon developed into a college for Welshmen: James Howell, Henry Vaughan, Evan Lloyd, Sir Lewis Morris, were among a number of later Anglo-Welsh poets to complete their education there. From both the schools and Jesus College a strong sense of Welshness emerges, but their vernacular was English.

"Wales England wed, so was I bred" wrote Ernest Rhys in his poem AUTOBIOGRAPHY (employing a line of the same length and structure as had been used by Sir Richard the Blackbird over three centuries before). What one Anglo-Welsh poet wrote of himself was substantially true of Anglo-Welsh poetry. It was a natural birth before Henry VIII's statute of Union, but that forced marriage bred the new literature in the nursery of the Tudor settlement of religion and education.

When, in his autobiographical poem I WAS BORN IN RHYMNEY, Idris Davies writes

> *I lost my native language*
> *For the one the Saxon spake*
> *By going to school by order*
> *For education's sake*

he is castigating what was for centuries the attitude of the schools of Wales to the Welsh language. Unwittingly he is also exposing their attitude, continued in their teaching to this day, to the English language. That the Saxon spake it is quite beside the point. The Irishman spake it as well; so did the American: and some Welshmen had spoken it—and written poetry in it—for at least four centuries. As early as 1558 the Denbigh-born, Oxford-educated Humphrey Llwyd (1527–1568) could refer—in his introduction to THE TREASVRI OF HELTH—to "our English tongue". The qualifying "English" clearly implies that there is another tongue, but the "our" recognizes a property in the English one. It had become a language of Wales (though "For education's sake" it has always been presented as the language of England).

The witness to this fact is that the English of the poems of Idris Davies, and of twentieth century Anglo-Welsh poetry in general, is the same, standard English (diversified in some cases, in rhyme and idiom, by the spoken English of modern Wales) of the Anglo-Welsh poets of the past. Few poets have employed any of the dialectal forms of English available in Wales.

The Tudor settlement created a professional class of Welshmen—parsons, physicians, lawyers, schoolmasters—literate in English and with leisure in which to write. But the English in which they wrote was in origin a second language—learnt, standard, correct; and they wrote it to be read by people like themselves. No doubt they often used Welsh for conversational purposes. Their English descended as a professional and literary language through a largely monoglot Welsh-speaking Wales. Unlike Scots English and Irish English, it was not the speech of the people. It has become such in the twentieth century, but the language of Anglo-Welsh poetry—handed down, perhaps, in the sacred arks of the physician Henry Vaughan and the parson George Herbert, who have continued to be read across the centuries—has remained the English of the professional class, from whom the overwhelming number of Anglo-Welsh poets from the sixteenth century until the present day have been drawn.

This is the strongest Anglo-Welsh tradition—the professional English of Anglo-Welsh poetry (though supported by the critical standpoint from which that language has often been handled, and by a recurrence of themes). In this—however unrealized by the poets themselves—lies the continuity with the past, the "connection with the far forefathers whose annals and epitaphs are the main substance of this essay". The English of twentieth century Anglo-Welsh poets is not the new language of many of the novelists and short-story writers.

Though poets and novelists may have received the same education, grown up in the same society, been exposed to the same influences, the Anglo-Welsh novel is essentially a twentieth century phenomenon, and its exponents have often felt free to write in an English which has become a new vernacular of Wales. However unaware of it, the poets have preserved and continued a linguistic tradition which goes back to the sixteenth century.

# IV

If the first Anglo-Welsh poem of which we have knowledge was a hymn to the queen of heaven, the next sustained achievement was a hymn to the queen of England—thus epitomizing one tendency to be observed in later Welsh history.

The poem is THE BLESSEDNES OF BRYTAINE, published in 1587, and in part called forth by a conspiracy of the previous year against Elizabeth in which two Welshmen had been implicated. Its thirty-three stanzas in praise of that queen are an echo in English of the bardic poetry of praise, celebrating a prince or patron. The poet, Morris Kyffin (*c.* 1555–1598), was born near Oswestry (Professor Glanmor Williams has noted that "of its 3,000 or so inhabitants most were Welsh in speech or origin"). Man of letters, translator, soldier, he wrote poetry in both languages and had studied in the bardic school of Wiliam Llŷn. Some of the stanzas are heavily alliterated, but the most interesting in terms of content are stanzas 31 and 32:

> *Ye Bryttish Poets, Repeat in Royall Song,*
> *(VVith waightie woords, vsed in King Arthurs daies)*
> *Th'Imperiall Stock, from whence your Queene hath sprong;*
> *Enstall in verse your Princesse lasting prayes:*
> *Pencerddiaid, play on Auncient Harp, and Crowde:*
> *Atceiniaid sing her prayses pearcing lowd.*

> *Let Hilles, & Rocks, rebounding Ecchoes yelde,*
> *Of Queene Elizabeths long lasting Fame;*
> *Let woody Groaues, and VVatry Streames be fild,*
> *And Creeks, & Caues, with sounding of the same:*
> *O Cambria, stretch, & straine thy vtmost breth,*
> *To praise, and pray for Queene Elizabeth.*

The Arthurian allusion and the appeal to the Pencerddiaid

(glossed in the margin as "Masters in the Science of Musick") and Atceiniaid ("Expert men in singing") establish the Welshness of the writer. Hills, rocks, creeks and caves, are hardly typical of the English countryside, and this is perhaps the first appearance of Welsh landscape in Anglo-Welsh poetry. It is interesting that the Arthurian and landscape elements are brought together in four lines of a contemporary poem, R. S. Thomas's A WELSHMAN TO ANY TOURIST:

> *The hills are fine, of course,*
> *Bearded with water to suggest age*
> *And pocked with caverns,*
> *One being Arthur's dormitory.*

A number of other Welshmen born in the sixteenth century published poetry in English. Sir John Stradling (1563–1637) of St Donat's, Glamorgan, was one of them: earlier in the century, a John Stradling, whose elegy was composed by one of the Tir Iarll poets, was celebrated as having mastered bardic knowledge, playing the harp, reading Welsh, and penillion singing, so the family cannot be dismissed as alien gentry.

Sir John Stradling's poem BEATI PACIFICI (1623) is a discursive meditation in more than 400 six-lined stanzas on the blessedness of peace-making. So early and genuine a preoccupation with this subject is interesting, for it was untypical of his time, though it looks forward to the Wales of Henry Richard, the nineteenth century "Apostle of Peace", and to the anti-militarist and passive resistance techniques which have on the whole characterized twentieth century Wales. The poem contains much curious knowledge, and some good lines. The fourteenth stanza has an almost medieval quality:

> *Christ when he came brought peace, and when he parted*
> *Left that behind to his Disciples deere:*
> *Their doctrine, vnto those whom they conuerted,*
> *Was full of peace: And whil'st they liued heere,*

*They taught vs still to pray*, Da pacem nobis,
*As Christ at parting say'd to them*, Pax vobis.

In stanza 223, in which he mentions himself, the writer emphasizes his Welshness by adding a gloss in the margin: "Cam(bro) Brit (annus). Glamorgan".

Another poet of this period was Hugh Holland (1569–1633) of Denbigh, traveller and man of letters, one of whose sonnets was prefaced to the First Folio of Shakespeare: it refers to "Britons brave" among the audiences at the Globe. A line elsewhere on the Anglesey-born Owen Tudor—"The man of Mone, magnifique Owen"—recalls the technical preoccupations within the line of earlier poets. Sir William Vaughan (1577–1641) of Gelli Aur, Carmarthenshire, educated at Jesus College, Oxford, founder of Cambriol—a colony in Newfoundland—was also reputed a good poet in English in his day, but his long work THE CHURCH MILITANT (1640) shows no good reason why.

Edward, Lord Herbert of Cherbury (1583–1648), in his autobiography—one of the earliest examples of the genre—records that "After I had attained the age of nine . . . my parents thought fit to send me to some place where I might learn the Welsh tongue, as believing it necessary to enable me to treat with those of my friends and tenants who understood no other language; whereupon I was recommended to Mr. Edward Thelwall, of Plas-y-ward in Denbighshire". In point of fact he was ill for the whole of his nine months' stay, but the intention was there. Since his younger brother George Herbert (1593–1633) also underwent instruction from a private tutor, possibly for the same purpose, any suggestion that these poets were Welsh only in name requires qualification.

George Herbert was probably born in Montgomery Castle, where grew THE PRIMROSE of Donne's poem. (Another of his poems— GOOD FRIDAY 1613—is connected with the same place: in one MS. copy the title is RIDING TO SIR EDWARD HERBERT IN WALES.)

Montgomery Castle must lie behind some of George Herbert's characteristic and precise images—those perhaps of real estate, furniture, hospitality, the winding stair, the quarry, gardening, riding, hawking, archery.

It must be said, though, that the only textual evidence of a sense of Welsh identity in THE TEMPLE (1633) is the title of one poem— THE BRITISH CHURCH. What makes this poem interesting—apart from its being a classical celebration of Anglicanism—is that a contemporary English poet would have entitled it THE ENGLISH CHURCH.

The Britain, Briton, British, characteristic of the diction of the early Anglo-Welsh poets, was in 1633 exclusive of the term English, not synonymous with it. In our own time it has fallen to R. S. Thomas further to purify the dialect of the tribe. His EXPATRIATES are defined as
> Not British; certainly
> Not English. Welsh
> With all the associations . . .

In George Herbert we see the preoccupation with form that has characterized Anglo-Welsh poetry from the beginning. The most striking examples of this are to be seen in his poems THE ALTAR and EASTER WINGS, where the pattern of the stanza is structured by syllabic and rhyme schemes into becoming a visual image of the title. The device has its ancestry in the Greek Anthology, but no doubt the geometrically shaped stanzas of Dylan Thomas's VISION AND PRAYER derive from Herbert's example. Formal experiment in a wider sense is seen in the circumstance that of the 164 poems in THE TEMPLE, 116 are said to be in forms which are not repeated.

Moreover, whatever its provenance, *dyfalu*—the heaping-up of comparisons—is exploited in a number of his poems: the first of the poems called PRAYER is a good example, with some 27 comparisons in one sonnet. The vividness of his images, the directness of his diction, the living speech-flow of his lines, all speak to the contemporary poet, and it is not surprising that R. S. Thomas should have edited A CHOICE OF GEORGE HERBERT'S VERSE.

Two other Anglo-Welsh poets born in the sixteenth century were James Howell (1594?–1666) and David Lloyd (1597–1663). Lloyd was born in Llanidloes, educated at Oxford, and became dean of St Asaph. His long poem THE LEGEND OF CAPTAIN JONES enjoyed great popularity, and was added to and reprinted a number of times. Said to be based on a Welsh poem—AWDL RICHARD JOHN GREULON, it creates a rumbustious hero who caught the imagination. His prowess is established in lines which preface Part I:

> 'Twas well the wars were done before
> Lost in Llewellin and Glendore.
> Had Jones liv'd then, in vain th' Assails
> Of Saxons; Wales had still been Wales.

His prowess was amatory as well as military, and the poem has a racy tone for a dean (until one recalls that Donne finished up as dean of St Paul's). The Captain is a picaresque hero—one of a long line that still flourishes at the present time—and his adventures were ubiquitous. At one stage in Part II he meets Prester John. The Ethiopian addresses him in grave Latin, which the Captain does not recognize and judges to be Arabic, intended to perplex him:

> Jones studying how t'express his eloquence
> In some strange language which might poze the prince,
> Now trouls him forth a full-mouth'd Welsh oration,
> Boldly deliver'd as became his Nation.
> The plot prov'd right, for not one word of sense
> Could be pickt from't, which vex'd the learned Prince . . .
> Jones hath his end, and then to make it known
> He had more tongues t'express himself than one,
> In a new tone he speaks, not half so rich,
> But better known, 'twas English . . .

James Howell was a parson's son, born at Cefn-bryn, Brecon-shire, educated at Jesus College, Oxford, who became historio-grapher-royal to Charles II of England. He was Welsh-speaking, and his Welshness accompanied him like a banner through life—and even after: Jacobus Howell, Cambro-Britannus opened his epitaph. At the same time he was a European man, a linguist and lexicographer. He contributed to Anglo-Welsh Literature in both prose and poetry, and his verse letter in 1629 to Ben Jonson Upon Dr. Davies' British Grammar is of interest as an early statement of a recurring theme in Anglo-Welsh poetry:

*This is the tongue the bards sung in of old,*
*And Druids their dark knowledge did unfold*

—the celebration in English of the Welsh language and its antiqu-ity and splendours. In the succession to James Howell's verses is R. S. Thomas's magnificent poem On Hearing a Welshman Speak, in which too the language contains the whole history of the nation that speaks it, and the further back one goes, the more triumphant and exultant that language and its life appear.

In some ways, however, the most interesting Anglo-Welsh poet to be born in the sixteenth century was John Davies.

# V

" 'Faith,' said Manawydan, 'we cannot live thus. Let us make for Lloegyr and seek some craft whereby we may make our livelihood.' They made for Lloegyr and came to Hereford."

So we read in the second branch of the MABINOGI, and such must also have been the experience of the forefathers of John Davies, who was born in Hereford about 1565 (and died in 1618). In Hereford at that time—as in Morris Kyffin's Oswestry—a good deal of Welsh was used, and for ecclesiastical purposes it is part of Wales to this day, lying within the archdiocese of Cardiff. The Welsh Marches have also given rise to at least one Anglo-Welsh novel of stature—the BORDER COUNTRY of Raymond Williams (himself a member of Yr Academi Gymreig, the Welsh Academy of Letters). John Davies was Welsh-speaking, and so completely was he identified with the land of his fathers that he was known as "The Welsh Poet"—though he generally designated himself "of Hereford".

In him the visual concern of George Herbert is given a different turn. The form that preoccupied him was, literally, the shape of the word, the drawing of speech—a form of reverence for language open to all the literate, though comparatively few care to practise it. Since things were much the same in his day, he was able to make a notable career as a writing-master: his penmanship brought him as pupils and friends some of the most illustrious in the England of his day. Like Hugh Holland, he appears to have known Shakespeare.

In 1878 Grosart raised the monument of THE COMPLETE WORKS OF JOHN DAVIES OF HEREFORD to his disastrous facility, in two hefty quarto volumes. In 1924 Hans Heidrich published in Berlin his JOHN DAVIES OF HEREFORD UND SEIN BILD VON SHAKESPEARE'S UMGEBUNG—an early example of the continuing Continental interest in Anglo-Welsh poetry. (Early studies of Dylan Thomas were undertaken in the Sorbonne and the University of Algiers, and in 1968 in the University of Toulouse and in 1969 in the Christian-Albrechts University at Kiel theses were submitted on R. S. Thomas.)

Here and there in John Davies's poems a good line stands out—"Loues language doth more Verbes then Nownes embrace" (one thinks of Dylan Thomas's "I learnt the verbs of will, and had my secret"): but the poem of most interest to Anglo-Welsh studies is CAMBRIA, written in 1603 to Henry Stuart, a Scot, called prince of Wales. In keeping with Davies's habitual prodigality it consists of 40 nine-lined stanzas, a number of which celebrate Wales and Welsh landscape and history—particularly its Trojan, Arthurian, and Tudor mutations ("Bosworth blind", in R. S. Thomas's neat phrase). The excesses to which we now know Croeso celebrations to be liable are interestingly anticipated in stanza 27, where the poet contemplates refurbishing the Roman legionary fortresses for a royal tour:

> *These will we now repaire, faire as before,*
> *That Scots, and Brittaines may mixt liue therein:*
> *Caerleon, where king Arthure liu'd of yore,*
> *Shall be rebuilt, and double gilt once more.*

The internal rhyme employed by earlier Anglo-Welsh poets persists here. What also persists—in Davies as in James Howell and Swrdwal—is a clear sense of superiority: the English are either ignored or patronized.

The most interesting lines are the concluding ones of stanza 35:

> *I speake for those, whose Tongues are strange to thee,*
> *In thine owne Tongue; if my words be vnfit,*
> *That blame be mine; but if Wales better be*
> *By my disgrace, I hold that grace to me.*

34

In making himself the spokesman for a Wales then largely Welsh-speaking, he is articulating for the first time one of the roles of the Anglo-Welsh poet—the interpretative, in which he speaks to an outside audience who know little or nothing of Wales. The other role—what might be called the reciprocal, where the poet speaks to the society which has produced him, the world of Wales—links earlier Anglo-Welsh poets with many contemporary ones.

Another Herefordshire Welshman was Rowland Watkyns, of whom we know little more than that he was born in Longtown— at that time part of the Anglican diocese of St David's, that he became vicar of Llanfrynach in Breconshire, and died in 1664. In 1968 Mr. Paul C. Davies and the University of Wales Press made Watkyns's book FLAMMA SINE FUMO (originally published in 1662) available again. He has neat lines—the opening of a poem on a Welsh judge, for example:

> Blush all you scarlet gowns, that heretofore
> Did wink at rich men, and condemn the poor.

He also has a certain epigrammatic power, as in the last lines of a poem on a Welsh country gentleman killed in battle:

> Now heaven crownes him, where all labours cease,
> Although he dy'd in war, he dy'd in peace.

Perhaps his best lines are on THE SHREW:

> Silence is her disease; for like a mill
> Her clapper goes, and never standeth still.
> By night Hobgoblins houses haunt: this sprite
> Doth vex and haunt the house both day and night.
> The Rack, the wheele, the Spanish Inquisition
> Torments not like her tongue . . .

Although at first sight the body of his poetry appears to have little to do with Wales, for like George Herbert's (with whom he shares an interest in herbalism) it is concerned with the universals of Christianity in their Anglican dress, it provides helpful information about the audience for whom he—and presumably other Anglo-Welsh poets of the time—were writing. Many of Watkyns's poems were addressed to a specific person, whose name and habitation appear at the head of the poem. This useful information suggests that the readership of Anglo-Welsh poetry was to be found, as one would expect, among the Welsh gentry and professional class—judges, soldiers, physicians and Anglican parsons. Like Welsh Literature in our own time, Anglo-Welsh Literature was in the nature of things written by a minority for a minority: but literatures do not depend upon a count of heads.

Watkyns—with George Herbert and David Lloyd—is one of a long line of Welsh Anglican parson poets. R. S. Thomas, a modern representative of their calling, has evoked it in his poem THE COUNTRY CLERGY:

> *I see th m working in old rectories*
> *By the sun's light, by candlelight,*
> *Venerable men, their black cloth*
> *A little dusty, a little green*
> *With holy mildew . . .*

# VI

In STUDIES IN LITERATURE (1919) Sir Arthur Quiller-Couch, then professor of English Literature in the University of Cambridge, made the following remark after a discussion of Thomas Traherne: "Before leaving him I will ask you to note that Donne, Herbert, Vaughan and he—the four whose spiritual kinship we have been tracing, came all by ancestry, proud or poor, from the Welsh Marches. Donne's forefathers were of Wales and spelt their name 'Dwynne'. The Herberts were lords over Pembroke, the Vaughans over Brecknockshire, Traherne a poor tradesman's son of Hereford. I distrust generalisations; but there would seem to be something here in 'the Celtic spirit'."

Of course this will not do, on all sorts of counts: unfortunately it has several times been advanced as a basis for Anglo-Welsh Literature. One has heard of a thesis attempted in the University of Wales on Welsh influences in the poetry of Donne, Herbert and Vaughan, which after three months' work got nowhere; and of an earlier thesis which was in the end rejected because the case was far from proved. This is not surprising. However, it has perhaps made the whole subject somewhat disreputable in the University of Wales, besides suggesting that the Anglo-Welsh case stands or falls by these names.

In 1952 Mr. Ioan Bowen Rees published an article entitled WALES AND THE ANGLO-WELSH, the English version of a paper originally delivered to the Dafydd ap Gwilym Society at Oxford. This paper embodies a vigorous attempt at the demolition of the Quiller-Couch line: "The first move of those who believed in Anglo-Welsh literature was to find a worthy tradition to include in their prospectus. Dead men tell no tales and many writers whose souls, even, cannot be considered Welsh were duly claimed. Quiller-Couch happened to remark at the end of one of his Cambridge lectures how four of the seventeenth century Metaphysicals had some connection with Wales—the Celtic temperament, no doubt. This casual observation seems to have been made the basis of the Anglo-Welsh heritage, in which Donne, a Londoner several generations removed from Wales, and Herbert, a Wiltshire country parson, who belonged to a family with estates in Wales, but with only a brief Welsh period between being de-anglicised and re-anglicised, reinforce the borderers Vaughan and Traherne. Now the coincidence of common ancestry and spiritual affinity in this group is undoubtedly curious, but, surely, too mystical to be brought into serious criticism, for a certain temperament is not the rigid monopoly of any one nation.'

As I have suggested, the Herberts cannot be so easily dismissed, and I hope it will appear that of the Welshness of Vaughan there can be no doubt. Though in an interim list called SEVENTY ANGLO-WELSH POETS, and published in 1954, I included Sir John Davies (to whom Quiller-Couch later drew attention as "another Welshman") and Donne and Traherne, it later became clear that no point was served in listing writers as Anglo-Welsh who were not Welsh-born and whose work showed no awareness of Wales. Sir John Davies came of a family that had settled in England in the Henry VII exodus; Traherne—though Quiller-Couch referred to him as "a poor Welsh parson"—was a borderer in several senses; and Donne was clearly a Londoner several generations removed from Wales. His influence is felt in the Anglo-Welsh poetry of the early seventeenth century—in George Herbert, Henry Vaughan, and Davies of Hereford (who knew him and has an epigram on him)—but he himself lies in the mainstream of English life and literature. Recent work suggests that all these poets were, in their "Divine Poems", writing a poetry of meditation inspired to some extent by Continental and Counter-Reformation methods, notably the Ignatian Exercises.

# VII

Morgan Llwyd (1619–1659) is one of a number of writers whose names are illustrious in the canon of literature in the Welsh language, but who also contributed to Anglo-Welsh Literature. In Morgan Llwyd's case this contribution was substantial both in quantity and in individuality. GWEITHIAU MORGAN LLWYD O WYNEDD (1899) gives 52 poems, 31 of which are in English, together with some English prose.

The exploration of Anglo-Welsh prose, apart from prose-fiction, has not yet begun; for that reason the present survey is almost exclusively of poetry, with an occasional mention of a landmark in prose. Reference to Morgan Llwyd's prose, puritan and apocalyptic, thus leads to the mention of another work of Anglo-Welsh religious prose of this time, the HOLY WISDOM of Dom Augustine Baker. Born David Baker (1575–1641) in Abergavenny, he became a Benedictine monk. HOLY WISDOM, a classic of the contemplative life, was published posthumously in 1657 and has been since reprinted.

Born at Cynfal, near Ffestiniog, Merioneth, Morgan Llwyd wandered hither and thither with the Parliamentary forces. Between 1645 and 1647 he spent time in London and came into contact with some of the religious and political leaders of the Civil War period. He came under the influence of the Quakers, the Fifth Monarchy Men, and the mysticism of Jacob Boehme. In 1647 he returned to Wrexham and devoted himself to preaching and writing.

His work is a poetry of protest—generally religious protest but sometimes social, as in the vigorous comment of

> *our King Queene Prince and Prelats high*
> *their merry Christmas spent*

> *with brawny hearts, when yet their dogs*
> *could lazarus lament.*

The stanza exemplifies the arbitrary punctuation and use of capitals in his poems, and the line division is sometimes haphazard—as though he in fact composes in long couplets but writes them down as quatrains in abcb, so that they have a ballad-like quality. Evidence for such a view is given in THE EXCUSE, where the lines are printed as long couplets:

> *All English swans that are alive and Scottish cuckowes*
> *sing*
> *and some Welsh swallowes chirpe and chime to welcome*
> *pleasant spring.*

His English, though powerful and vivid, was clearly a second language, and on occasion he concludes with a couplet in Welsh or introduces a Welsh phrase, as in

> *Brave Hugonits, stiffe Mordecais, stout lol-*
> *lards you stood fast*
> *a glana iw'r gelynen wyrdd that scornd the*
> *Romish blast*

—which well illustrates his arbitrary line division.

The vigour and directness of Morgan Llwyd's poems are due technically to his use of a diction drawn from the Germanic side of English, thus short and concrete words, and an imagery based on the Bible and on common life—sleep, eating and drinking, dancing, weather, the seasons, the stable, the farmyard. He also employs the seventeenth century image of the voyages of discovery—"Our northeast cutt to Indies mines"—applying it to the Reformation.

In construction there is a frequent but vivid use of Biblical phrase:

> *Their puffs blew downe the christian trees,*
> *five thousand every day.*
> *They crye. Their blood upon us bee. Away*
> *with them Away*

and a use, sometimes heady, of alliteration and internal rhyme:

> *My love, my light, my song, my sight, my bread,*
> *my bright eternall one*
> *Hee doth not cease, to give increase, with Peace*
> *and ease in one*

is reminiscent in this respect of the last stanza of the HYMN TO THE VIRGIN. The rhyming of *ease* with *cease/ increase/ Peace* is an early recording of the pronunciation of the Z sound as a sibilant in English as a language of Wales, which affects Anglo-Welsh rhyme into the twentieth century: W. H. Davies rhymes *gas* with *has.*

Sometimes Morgan Llwyd's apocalyptic vision is lyrical:

> *Sing on a brittle sea of glasse*
> *Sing in a furne of fire*
> *In flames wee leap for joy and find*
> *a cave a singing quire*

but more often it chants magnificent anthemas. His priorities are clear:

> *Lett Wales & England rowzed bee,*
> *O churches, sleep no more.*

Committed, passionate, intense, he hurls prophetic thunderbolts abroad and with tender lyricism comforts Wales:

> *Come downe O London to the dust*
> *lett Christ sitt on the throne*
> *And bee not drunke with witt and wealth*
> *Else sitt with Tyre alone.*

41

*O Wales, poor Rachel, thou shalt beare*
*sad Hannah now rejoyce*
*The last is first, the summer comes*
*to heare the turtles voice.*

Like James Howell, Morgan Llwyd is a European man—though so far as is known he never set foot on the Continent. However, from his meeting house in Wrexham he gazes out on time and space, his panoramic vision ranging from 1652 to judgment day, from Wales to Holland, France, Germany; and in a stanza of intricate assonances he summons Europe to doom:

*Wo is to Europe. Now the day*
*approacheth very nigh*
*Of plague, flame, sword, & hailstones great*
*Wo Europe blind and high.*

With its simplicity of form, its social and religious protests, its vision of Europa Deserta, Europe made a spiritual desert, Morgan Llwyd's poetry strikes a note in Anglo-Welsh Literature which is not to be heard again until our own century—in the GWALIA DESERTA of Idris Davies, and thereafter in THE GREEN DESERT of Harri Webb.

# VIII

Morgan Llwyd's longest poem—from which a number of the examples given above were drawn—appears to be called simply *1648:* there is a certain arbitrariness about his titles as well as his line-lengths, and often—as with Dylan Thomas—the title is the first line of the poem. At all events, about 1648 another Welshman underwent a formative religious experience. Writing about it later, Henry Vaughan the Silurist confessed that "The first that with any effectual success attempted a diversion of this foul and overflowing stream" (he is referring to his love poetry) "was the blessed man Mr. George Herbert, whose holy life and verse gained many pious Converts (of whom I am the least)."

Both Vaughan and Herbert were descendants of that "Davy Gam, esquire" who is named as an Agincourt casualty in HENRY V, act 5, scene 8. Though they were only distantly related by blood (and there was a wide gap between their ages—Vaughan was only twelve when Herbert died), they were so closely related by poetry that many of Vaughan's titles (he too has a BRITTISH CHURCH), and some of his lines, echo those of THE TEMPLE.

Henry Vaughan (1621–1695) was born in Trenewydd, Breconshire, and educated at Jesus College, Oxford. Canon F. E. Hutchinson, editor of both Vaughan and Herbert, has called him "The most Welsh of all who have written English poetry"— thus demonstrating the curious and widespread tendency of many critics to pontificate on Anglo-Welsh matters out of an almost total ignorance of the facts. However, that Vaughan was Welsh-speaking is not in doubt: he needed to be in order to carry on his practice as a physician in rural Breconshire. There is in any case clear textual evidence: his twin brother Thomas (who also wrote poetry) said of himself "English is a language the author was not born to", and the Silurist once uses a Welsh quotation—attributed to Aneirin. But it is that epithet—which he attaches to his name on the title-page of SILEX SCINTILLANS (1650) and on his tomb-stone—which shows his clear intention of advertising himself to be a Welshman, a descendant of the Silures who so fiercely resisted the Roman invasion of their territory around the Usk.

Vaughan is concerned with the same universals of religious experience as George Herbert and Rowland Watkyns, though in a very different way: his is that poetry of lyrical abstractions, of light and darkness, which we meet in our own time in the work of Vernon Watkins. As to elements deriving from Wales, it has been suggested that his distinctive use of the epithet white draws on the wider values of the word *gwyn* in Welsh. There is a characteristic use of alliteration and assonance, and in a poem like SONDAYES we see the heaping-up of comparisons—*dyfalu*—which was referred to in Herbert. A contemporary Anglo-Welsh poet from Breconshire, Roland Mathias, has discussed why Vaughan—living much of his life in the magnificent and distinctive scenery of that region—should have reduced it to a conventional diction of streams, groves, fountains and rocks. He suggests that it represents an attempt to present Wales in the fashionable terms of classical urbanity. "We like Civilitie" Davies of Hereford had written in 1603 in his CAMBRIA, and this attitude was to characterize Anglo-Welsh poetry to the end of the following century. Nonetheless, however Virgillian the convention, there is to the outsider a clear sense of the mountains, oaks, waters, of Brecon-shire in Vaughan's poetry—and above all of Isca, the Usk.

The poem in which this river is most vividly present is THE WATER-FALL, which is at the same time a celebration of the Usk and an allegory of life. The structural complexity of the first stanza, with its alternation of long and short couplets, is clearly designed to convey through the movement of the verse the movement of water approaching a waterfall:

> *With what deep murmurs through times silent stealth*
> *Doth thy transparent, cool and watry wealth*

*Here flowing fall,*
*And chide, and call,*
*As if his liquid, loose Retinue staid*
*Lingring, and were of this steep place afraid,*
*The common pass*
*Where, clear as glass,*
*All must descend*
*Not to an end:*
*But quickned by this deep and rocky grave,*
*Rise to a longer course more bright and brave.*

The narrowing and the increasing speed of the river is conveyed through the contraction of the first long couplet into the second short one, and the third couplet observantly records the way this swift movement is slowed down (as is the verse) and the water appears to hesitate on the lip of the fall. Four short lines convey the smooth descent of the water as it falls, and the concluding long couplet returns the river to a slow movement at its new level. The remainder of the poem is in octosyllabic couplets, as in its new channel the slightly swifter but now untroubled flow of the water allows the allegorical implications glimpsed in the first stanza to be revealed. Like Dylan Thomas, Vaughan opens

*the leaves of the water at a passage*
*Of psalms and shadows,*

drawing upon the archetypal values of water in the scriptures as a symbol of life, of purity, and of freedom.

With a percipience, prompted by the present state of Wales, of new relevances and validities (evident also in his own poetry), Harri Webb has suggested an interesting contemporary reading of THE WATER-FALL. In a Wales in which calculated inundation, reservoirs perpetrated and threatened, pipelines likewise, and the compulsory export of water, have become the images most immediately related to national integrity—in the Wales of Mr.

Huw Jones's popular song Dŵr—THE WATER-FALL has become ; political poem.

After it, for contrast, should be read one of the most vigorous poems to come out of modern Breconshire—Roland Mathias's THE FLOODED VALLEY.

## IX

"There are not more than half a dozen Welsh poets who wrote in English of any genuine importance between 1622, when Henry Vaughan was born, and 1944 when Alun Lewis died, though there are many able and charming writers." Vaughan was in fact born in 1621, and the present essay has attempted to put forward some evidence to refute the implication that Anglo-Welsh Literature began then: there is also the question of what is meant by "any genuine importance". Nonetheless, Dylan Thomas's remark is interesting—not least because it shows that he thought about such matters, was aware of an Anglo-Welsh Literature and, by implication, of himself as a part of it. The quotation is taken from the published version of a broadcast poetry reading which he introduced and delivered: the poets represented are Vaughan, Edward Thomas, W. H. Davies, Idris Davies, Glyn Jones, and Alun Lewis. John Dyer and Sir Lewis Morris were also mentioned.

His selection (in 1946) of this sequence of poets, his recognition of common elements linking them, makes one contemplate with renewed wonder the blithe assumption of some Anglo-American criticism that Dylan Thomas's own poetry might as easily have been composed in Swanage or Sewanee as in Swansea. Its virtuoso "craft or art", characteristic of Anglo-Welsh poetry from the beginning; its use of *proest, cymeriadau*, modified *cynghanedd;* its topography, and the allusions that derive from it (the larger-than-life MABINOGI "in the tall tales/Beyond the border" of Pembrokeshire, across which the road from Laugharne leads up to Narberth): all these illuminate the observation in THE TIMES obituary (written by Vernon Watkins) that "It was, even in its first phases, an ancient poetry, not rejecting antiquity for the present but seeking, with every device of language, the ancestry of the moment".

But to return to Dylan Thomas's comment on Anglo-Welsh

poetry: it is impossible within the limits of this brief survey to do justice to the "many able and charming writers" between Henry Vaughan and the beginning of the twentieth century—partly because there are so many of them. Brief biographical and bibliographical details of a number of them will be found in section XIX, but the list given there should certainly not be considered exhaustive. The remainder of this essay will be selective to a much greater degree, drawing attention to Anglo-Welsh poets of the eighteenth and nineteenth centuries with whom the reader may not be familiar. However, the cumulative significance of the archive of Anglo-Welsh poets down the ages should not be ignored. In the mysterious economy of poetry, it seems that for the few to be chosen, many must be called. Moreover, T. S. Eliot has drawn attention to the need for a criticism which "will be able to sweep the distance and gain an acquaintance with minute objects in the landscape with which to compare minute objects close at hand". In TRADITION AND THE INDIVIDUAL TALENT he stresses that no poet has his complete meaning alone: "His significance, his appreciation is the appreciation of his relation to the dead poets and artists. You cannot value him alone; you must set him, for contrast and comparison, among the dead". And lest such work should be dismissed as mere literary archaeology, he adds: "I mean this as a principle of aesthetic, not merely historical, criticism".

# X

In a recent poem—A SENSE OF PLACE—John Stuart Williams, whose poetry is concerned above all with the precise evocation of place at home and abroad, has made this comment on Welsh topography:

> *The contours of this map*
> *are a definition, a firm*
> *placement of sea and land:*
> *we know where we stand.*

This sense of what Eliot has called "a particular people in a particular place" is very strong in Anglo-Welsh Literature. Though the elements are present in earlier poems, it is in the eighteenth century that Welsh landscape emerges as one of the major themes of Anglo-Welsh poetry from that time onwards. One of the earliest examples of its treatment is that by John Dyer (1699–1757), a Carmarthenshire man who eventually became an Anglican clergyman. Before this he was a painter, and it is with a painter's awareness of colour and perspective that he writes of GRONGAR HILL (1727) in the Tywi valley:

> *Below me trees unnumber'd rise,*
> *Beautiful in various dyes;*
> *The gloomy pine, the poplar blue,*
> *The yellow beech, the sable yew,*
> *The slender fir, that taper grows,*
> *The sturdy oak with broad-spread boughs,*
> *And beyond the purple grove,*
> *Haunt of Phyllis, queen of love!*
> *Gaudy as the op'ning dawn,*
> *Lies a long and level lawn,*
> *On which a dark hill, steep and high,*
> *Holds and charms the wand'ring eye.*

It is noteworthy that the most lyrical poetry of place in modern

Anglo-Welsh poetry has come from a few miles down river from Grongar Hill. From the two west Carmarthenshire peninsulas, on the estuaries of the Tywi and the Tâf, come Dylan Thomas's FERN HILL (Llangain, on the road to Llansteffan) and POEM IN OCTOBER and OVER SIR JOHN's HILL (Laugharne).

All the Anglo-Welsh landscape poems of the eighteenth century embody the two qualities of Welsh landscape which form the theme of R. S. Thomas's poem of that title. There is

> *the past,*
> *Brittle with relics,*
> *Wind-bitten towers and castles;*

and the sense of desolation:

> *There are cries in the dark at night*
> *As owls answer the moon,*
> *And thick ambush of shadows,*
> *Hushed at the fields' corners.*

Having introduced his castle, Dyer evokes its present condition:

> *Tis now the raven's bleak abode;*
> *'Tis now th'apartment of the toad;*
> *And there the fox securely feeds,*
> *And there the pois'nous adder breeds,*
> *Conceal'd in ruins, moss and weeds.*

In Evan Evans (with whom this essay began) there is again a combination of the past and of desolation—in A PARAPHRASE OF PSALM CXXXVII (1772):

> *No more shall Mona's oaks be spar'd,*
> *Or Druid circle be rever'd.*
> *On Conway's banks and Menai's streams*
> *The solitary bittern screams;*
> *And, where was erst Llywelyn's Court,*
> *Ill-omen'd birds and wolves resort.*

Mr. Saunders Lewis has pointed out that though the bittern comes from Goldsmith's DESERTED VILLAGE (1770) and an "Eagle screams and passes by" in Gray's THE BARD (1757), "yet it is well to remember that this mood of lament, which for a moment links Goldsmith with Gray and Ossian, was long familiar to Evans in Welsh literature. It is the mood of much of the oldest Welsh poetry".

Edward Davies (1718–1789)—like the preceding poets an Anglican clergyman—published his long work CHEPSTOW; A POEM in 1784. As a labour of love, Mr. Ivor Waters of the Chepstow Society caused this to be reprinted in 1952, and in 1967 published an elegant booklet of selections from it, with illustrations. Canto IV is of interest in that it records the state of Tintern Abbey nine years before Wordsworth's first visit:

> *Here now no bell calls monks to morning pray'r,*
> *Daws only chant their early matins here;*
> *Black forges smoke, and noisy hammers beat,*
> *Where sooty cyclops, puffing, drink and sweat;*
> *Confront the curling flames, nor back retire,*
> *But live, like salamanders, in the fire*

—perhaps the first appearance in Anglo-Welsh Literature of the industrial themes which are to characterize it in the first half of the twentieth century, (above all in the novel, but also in the poems of Idris Davies and, more recently, those of Robert Morgan and Alan Perry). But the most vigorous lines in the poem are a description of foxhunting in the Wye valley:

> *Here, in the hollow caverns of the rocks,*
> *Skulks, in security, the wily fox:*
> *Snug, in his fronzy kennel, Reynard lies,*
> *And all the snares of men and dogs defies.*
> *In vain the hounds attempt to storm his cave—*
> *Some enter, but, alas! there find a grave;*
> *Some tumble down the rocks, and perish in the wave.*
> *Confusion reigns, enraged, the baying pack,*
> *Loud and more loud renews the vain attack.*
> *In vain the huntsmen shout, and wind the horn—*
> *The fox, triumphant, laughs them all to scorn.*

Fifteen years later, and at the other end of Wales, Richard Llwyd (1752–1835)—called "The Bard of Snowdon"—celebrated the beauties of Anglesey. Yet his long poem BEAUMARIS BAY (1800) offers the same conjunction of the gothic and the desolation of nature as Dyer's poem nearly three-quarters of a century earlier:

> *Alas! what is it now? the damp abode*
> *Of slimy snails, the spider, and the toad;*
> *Where waking owls in screaming concert call*
> *Their prowling mates, when evening's shadows fall.*

This state of affairs at Penmon Priory is contrasted with the gardens of Lord Bulkeley's house, Baron-Hill, where the Muse, Flora, Dryads and Satyrs are all to be observed (just as Dyer noted Phyllis in the Tywi valley). The description ends with a couplet of pleasant but unintended ambiguity:

> *For Art and Nature here their beauties blend,*
> *And Taste and Bulkeley for the palm contend.*

Like the pastoral, the occasional poetry of desolation no doubt represents an escape from a life which has become urbane, domesticated and secure. The Civil Wars of the seventeenth century had passed out of living memory, the industrial wars of the nineteenth century cast no shadows yet; Rebecca would not ride until 1839; these eighteenth century poets rode out to experience their pleasant *frisson* of desolation through a Wales at peace—which the bulk of the lines in their poems celebrates.

Ironically enough, their abominations of desolation—Dyer's Dynevor, Evan Evans's Conway and Dolwyddelan, Davies's Tintern and Llwyd's Penmon—are now places which (like R. S. Thomas AT ST JAMES'S PARK) we are invited to enter as one of the public, there to conduct ourselves in accordance with the regulations. So successfully have the valleys been exalted by the tourist advertisements, and the mountains and hills made low, the crooked made straight, and the rough places plain, by the county councils, that the passing of wild Wales has become one of the themes of contemporary Anglo-Welsh poetry.

# XI

Just as R. S. Thomas's WELSH LANDSCAPE evokes history, so his
WELSH HISTORY evokes landscape:

> *Our kings died, or they were slain*
> *By the old treachery at the ford.*
> *Our bards perished, driven from the halls*
> *Of nobles by the thorn and bramble.*

Welsh history is as much the concern of Davies of Hereford's
CAMBRIA, and of Evan Evans, Edward Davies and Richard
Llwyd, as Welsh landscape is. The past is a constant theme,
triumphant and golden. While a more critical view of the past is
to be found in contemporary poets like Roland Mathias, Harri
Webb and John Tripp, who have frequently taken aspects of
Welsh history as their theme, the charge has been several times
levelled against modern Anglo-Welsh Literature that it is too
preoccupied with the past. If more is intended by this than a
stricture upon a too easy nostalgia (against which must be set,
in any case, a considerable number of poems which are patently
concerned with the only too vivid present), then one value of the
study of earlier Anglo-Welsh Literature becomes evident. It
shows that a preoccupation with the past is not necessarily a
modern malaise but a recurrent theme over the centuries. Some
indeed might see in this one of the expected and defining characteristics of Anglo-Welsh Literature. In his replies to the WALES
Questionnaire of 1946, R. S. Thomas wrote that—to the artist—a
consciousness of Wales should involve "the constant realization
that he lives in or belongs to a country of great age, that by
geography and tradition has developed an individual way of life,
and that his chief duty as an artist is to beautify, to purify and to
enlarge that way of life. After all, why chant the praise of Helen,
when Nêst remains unsung? Why lament Troy fallen, when
Mathrafal lies in ruins?" The most sustained manifestation of the

consciousness of belonging to "a country of great age" is the art of David Jones. It is also to be seen clearly in the work of Anthony Conran and Gwyn Williams, and in John Ormond's magnificent poem ANCIENT MONUMENTS.

When James Howell and Davies of Hereford look at the role of their nation in history, they are in no doubt that they are the top people. Right at the beginning, Swrdwal's HYMN TO THE VIRGIN was intended to demonstrate the same thing. The attitude summed up in Milton's "An old and haughty Nation proud in Arms" persists right through the eighteenth century. There is an interesting contrast between a passage in R. S. Thomas's WELSH HISTORY and one in Edward Davies's CHEPSTOW. Here is the poem of 1952:

> We were a people bred on legends,
> Warming our hands at the red past.
> The great were ashamed of our loose rags
> Clinging stubbornly to the proud tree
> Of blood and birth, our lean bellies
> And mud houses were a proof
> Of our ineptitude for life.

And the passage of 1784:

> Where cider ends there ale begins to reign,
> And warms on Brecknock hills the Cambrian swain;
> High on the summit of King Arthur's Chair
> He quaffs his ale, and breathes untainted air;
> Looks down on Hereford with scornful eyes—
> Esteems himself a native of the skies:
> Puff'd with the thoughts of his exalted birth
> He scorns the humble mushroom sons of earth;
> His high descent from time's first dawn can trace,
> From Gomer down to Owen Tudor's race;
> Thinks none so great on this terraqueous ball—
> Himself the ragged emperor of all.

*This mountain prince outflies ballooning Kings,*
*A cloud his car—the winds his whistling wings.*

Both depict a ragged forefather of Iago Prytherch, but Davies's peasant is magnificently contemptuous of the judgments and pretensions of others.

A final contrast will make clear the extent of the collapse when it came. Mr. Gerald Morgan has prefaced a note on an unidentified bilingual poet writing shortly after 1688, whom he has called the Brogyntyn Poet, with a quotation from his poem ON THE WELCH:

*The guile and softness of the Saxon race*
*In gallant Briton's soul had never place;*
*Strong as his rocks, and in his language pure,*
*In his own innocence and truth secure:*
*Such is the bold, the noble mountaineer.*

In 1864 T. Hughes—an Anglican parson from Denbighshire who published his own and his father's verses in Welsh, Latin and English, in a volume laconically entitled POEMS BY HUGHES—wrote his own poem, SNOWDON, about the "mountaineers" of north Wales. Towards the end of it occur these lines:

*Nurs'd in thy fastness, mountain, King of Wales,*
*Her language yet shall die within thy dales.*
*All-conquering English rushes on apace;*
*Railways already drive it to thy base:*
*Soon, shall "Dim Saesneg" be a sound gone by,*
*And, like the echoes of the breezes, die.*
*'Tis well 'twere so! the people now are one,*
*Need but one tongue to work in unison.*

The death-wish has come, apparently with the increase in tourism (the Treachery of the Blue Books had come in 1847). This represents the nadir, both in verse and attitude, of that treatment of the Welsh language as a theme of Anglo-Welsh poetry which began with James Howell's poem of 1629 UPON DR. DAVIES' BRITISH GRAMMAR. It represents the state of mind in the schools of Wales at the time that Idris Davies castigates in I WAS BORN IN RHYMNEY. Like him, contemporary Anglo-Welsh poets have sided with James Howell. Indeed, for Emyr Humphreys—in the moving peroration to his poem ANCESTOR WORSHIP—Welsh is like a force of nature, and will endure as long as the ocean:

> The air is still committed to their speech
> Their voices live in the air
> Like leaves like clouds like rain
> Their words call out to be spoken
> Until the language dies
> Until the ocean changes.

Hughes's lines record the *trahison des clercs*, the abandonment of bilingualism by the professional class, a process which has only begun to be reversed in our own day. However, Keidrych Rhys observes in one of his poems that "The strength of the common man was always the strength of Wales", and at about the same time as Hughes was writing, a working-man—John Jones (1788–1858) of Llanasa, Flint, called "Poet Jones"—records a different picture in another social class. In his eighth year he was apprenticed to a cotton-spinner in Holywell, where he learned to read and write, and in his poem HOLYWELL occurs this vigorous evocation of a street scene in that town:

> 'Tis market day;—loud dealers strain their lungs,
> And High-street echoes with two different tongues.
> The Welsh and English there alternate cry,
> "Rhai'n, rhai'n, yw pethau rhad"—"come buy, come buy!"

# XII

At least four women published Anglo-Welsh poetry in the eighteenth century—Jane Brereton, born Hughes (1685–1740) of Bryn Griffith, near Mold; Anna Williams (1706–1783) of Rosemarket, Pembrokeshire, who lived in Dr. Johnson's household for the last thirty years of her life; Anne Penny (fl. 1729–1780); and Julia Ann Hatton (1764–1838).

Anne Penny was also born Hughes, probably in Bangor, the daughter of a clergyman. After her marriage she lived in London, and there she published several volumes. Her POEMS (1780) form a large and handsome leather-bound volume: only the inmate does not correspond. The poems are copious and of a vapidity so sustained as to be in itself a remarkable negative achievement. The first two are in some remote sense "from the Welsh"—TALIESIN'S POEM TO PRINCE ELPHIN and AN ELEGY ON NEEST, thus spelt. The plethora of abstractions and personifications approaches health of language only once, in the opening stanza of POEM XXVI:

> *As I sat, with my beautiful lass,*
> *Where Lillies, and Roses did grow;*
> *She pluck'd up a Sprig of the Grass,*
> *Which she threw, on the Valley below.*

The last line records the only behaviour reminiscent of real experience in the entire book, and the grass is in fact cast into an oven of lukewarm metaphors and wilts away into allegory.

If Anna Williams and Anne Penny gravitated towards London, Julia Ann Hatton gravitated away from it—on one occasion as far as America, but latterly to Swansea and Cydweli. The impulse behind these Welsh permutations was the great Mrs. Siddons, her elder sister—for Julia Ann, though she became successively Curtis and Hatton, was born Kemble. According to the DICTIONARY OF NATIONAL BIOGRAPHY, "Great annoyance was caused to the actress by the proceedings of her sister Ann . . . who read lectures at Dr. Graham's Temple of Health, led a discreditable career, attempted to poison herself in Westminster Abbey, made appeals to the public, and announced herself everywhere as the youngest sister of Mrs. Siddons".

It is said that the actress made her an allowance of £20 a year on condition that she lived a hundred and fifty miles from London, and so perhaps her sterling area began at Swansea—where, with her husband Hatton, she kept the Swansea Bathing House. After his death she moved to Cydweli, where she kept a dancing-school. We are told that between 1815 and 1831 she wrote at least a dozen novels.

It was, however, as "Ann of Swansea" that she published her two volumes of poetry. The second has a throw-away title, POETIC TRIFLES (1811), which is unfortunately only too apt, though the first—POEMS ON MISCELLANEOUS SUBJECTS (1783)—is said to be worse. One regrets that this startling, spirited, eccentric woman— so vivid in the awed animadversions of others upon her highly individual conduct—should have been totally incapable of conveying any of this through her own written words. Her poem SWANSEA BAY is said to be above the average, but few remarks could be more discouraging for it is a classical model of the bad poem. So unerringly does it fail in terms of statement, form, diction, construction, imagery, that it has a certain interest and function as an awful example. The fourth stanza is marginally less bad than the other seven:

> *' Tis not for me the snowy sail*
> *Swells joyous in the balmy gale;*
> *Nor cuts the boat with frolic play*
> *For me the waves of Swansea Bay.*

SWANSEA BAY is a poem that sends the reader, on the one hand, to Vernon Watkins's magnificent ODE TO SWANSEA:

*Bright town, tossed by waves of time to a hill,*
*Leaning Ark of the world, dense-windowed, perched*
*High on the slope of morning,*
*Taking fire from the kindling East . . .*

*Stone-runged streets ascending to that crow's nest*
*Swinging East and West over Swansea Bay*
*Guard in their walls Cwmdonkin's*
*Gates of light for a bell to close.*

It sends one as well to the Anglo-Welsh poetry written in the
twentieth century by women—in particular to Brenda Chamberlain, to Gillian Clarke's exact insights into places and common-
places, to Ruth Bidgood's articulation of vulnerability, and to
Sally Roberts and her memorable celebration of the eighteenth
century Welsh mystic ANN GRIFFITHS in a poem of that title:

*My songs as light as ash are spent;*
*My hope's elsewhere, a long descent*
*In flesh and land—and yet the air*
*Stirs with fresh music, calls me where*
*Intricate webs of words begin.*

*Lord, let me not be silent till*
*All earth is grinding in Your mill!*

# XIII

One of the recurring themes of Anglo-Welsh poetry is a pre-occupation with the metaphysical, in one or other of the various senses of the term—from the HYMN TO THE VIRGIN, through Herbert, Watkyns, Vaughan, Morgan Llwyd, to Dylan Thomas's VISION AND PRAYER and the poetry of Vernon Watkins and David Jones's ANATHEMATA (which consists of thoughts stirred in the mind, as often as not, "in the time of the Mass").

Another of the recurrent marks of Anglo-Welsh poetry throughout its whole course is a preoccupation with form, with "craft or art", with the wrought word and its sonic and visual properties. Another is a continuity of the themes of Welsh history, Welsh landscape and topography, the Welsh language—and the theme of the analysis and significance of Welshness in terms beyond these: what R. Gerallt Jones in a recent poem (about the colour problem) has called being "coloured Welsh in this grey mould of Europe".

It may be said that English poetry also offers recurrent examples of preoccupation with form, with the history, topography and language of England; that it is all, implicitly or explicitly, about the nature of Englishness. As an argument against a distinct Anglo-Welsh Literature this is not valid—first because the emphases differ considerably; and second because all literatures are about what it is like to be a human being, a creature defined by a history, topography and language, and differ only in emphasis. Every literature, in short, is about its own modulation of a common subject-matter, the human condition.

To invalidate Anglo-Welsh Literature it is necessary to demonstrate that, like Hardy's Wessex and Wordsworth's Lake District, the Wales articulated in the English language is essentially another western, regional modulation of the English norm. That Anglo-

Welsh Literature grew up, through several centuries, in a close awareness of Welsh Literature and the Welsh language; that it articulates a human situation with a history, allegiances, emphases, different from those of an English region: all this would have to be disproved, or proved irrelevant. In contemporary Wales these emphases might seem to underline a highly verbal culture, the minimising of class distinction, and a rigorous commitment to non-violence in spite of all provocation: all of which are reflected in contemporary Anglo-Welsh Literature.

To return to the metaphysical theme, in the sense of a concern with the supernatural and the visionary: in the eighteenth century this expresses itself in Anglo-Welsh poetry, as in Welsh, in the composition of hymns. Peter Williams (1723–1796), a Methodist minister from Llansadyrnin, Carmarthenshire, published HYMNS ON VARIOUS SUBJECTS (1771) as well as his hymns in the Welsh language. William Williams (1717–1791), Pantycelyn, published a collection of hymns in English—HOSANNA TO THE SON OF DAVID (1759)—most of which were original compositions, not translations of his Welsh hymns. HYMN XIX has a fine stanza, reminiscent of the world of light and darkness of Henry Vaughan:

> O! let me see those beams of light,
> Feel that celestial spark
> That veils the beauties of the world
> In an eternal dark.

HYMN XXXII also has a memorable stanza:

> The Moon and all her train surrounding,
> With the lofty dazzling Sun,
> Now are wearied in the heavens
> Their laborious course to run;
> Earth and sea in mighty travail
> With their creatures never cease,
> Groaning for the revelation,
> Glorious, of the sons of peace.

In 1772 appeared GLORIA IN EXCELSIS, an English set of the hymns published in Welsh in 1771 and 1772, and some of these remind us that English was Pantycelyn's second language. HYMN XCIII has a wrong sequence of tenses:

> *Now the shadows flee and vanish,*
> *And the blessed morning* came

and HYMN LXIII gives plural verbs to a singular subject:

> *When every vail that stands between*
> Are *rent, and never more* are *seen.*

I am indebted to my colleague the Revd. Islwyn Jenkins for the information that the quatrains in which Idris Davies often wrote show the influence of hymnody upon him, and this must be true of a number of other Anglo-Welsh writers.

# XIV

Among the best things in twentieth century Anglo-Welsh poetry are the memorable portraits of Welsh men and women. The most sustained achievement in this field is the sequence of eighteen poems, spread over twenty-three years, which delineate R. S. Thomas's Iago Prytherch—a monoglot English-speaking, Manafon countryman (strangely misread in Bryn Griffiths's poem THE MASTER), and thus one extreme of the Anglo-Welsh spectrum—which is represented at the other by the situation of Morgan Llwyd. The particular interest of these poems is that they construct portraits of two Welshmen who compel our gaze—Iago Prytherch and his creator.

The portrait poem originates in the eighteenth century, and one of the earliest examples is by Lewis Morris (1701–1765)—Llewelyn Ddu o Fôn. Born in the appropriately and beautifully named parish of Llanfihangel Tre'r Beirdd, Anglesey, he became one of the most distinguished Welsh scholars and poets of the century. In a letter to an English antiquary, Morris went to some pains to understate his control of the English language. Mr. Saunders Lewis has drawn attention to a probable element of ruse in this letter, and is inclined to endorse Iolo Morganwg's statement that "Lewis Morris has been more thoroughly educated in the English language than most." At all events, his poem THE FISHING LASS OF HAKIN (near Milford Haven) shows a vigorous control of English. In one way it is reminiscent of one of the best known modern portrait poems, THE HUNCHBACK IN THE PARK of Dylan Thomas, who

> *Made all day until bell time*
> *A woman figure without fault.*

To some extent Morris's poem is a parody of popular ballads of the time, but it exists in its own right as a poem and as a portrait, vivid, rollicking, audacious:

> *Her cheeks are as a mackrel plump,*
> *No mouth of mullet moister;*
> *Her lips of tench would make you jump,*
> *They open like an oyster;*
> *Her chin as smooth as river trout,*
> *Her hair as rockfish yellow:*
> *Cod's Sounds, I viewed her round about*
> *But never saw her fellow.*

"A man of genius, and a Welch man"—the words are David Garrick's, and they form the title of Professor Cecil Price's Inaugural Lecture at Swansea in 1963. Evan Lloyd (1734–1776), to whom the words apply, was born at Bala, Merioneth, educated at Jesus College, Oxford, and became a convivial clergyman with a penchant for penillion singing. Between 1766 and 1768 he published four long poems, one of which—THE CURATE—gives a satirical portrait of a bishop:

> *He in Christ's doctrine deals, by way of trade,*
> *Money by preaching poverty is made—*
> *Whose labours were bestow'd upon the head,*
> *Whose heart, that found itself neglected, fled,*
> *And now a mere, mere head he lives, with Greek*
> *Carv'd on his skull, and furrow'd in his cheek;*
> *Be-greek'd, be-latin'd, and be-hebrew'd too,*
> *Yet from no tongue has learnt what he should do.*

The satirical portrait today is well seen in Herbert Williams's slight, sharp sketch LIKE FATHER? John Ormond's fine poem THE AMBUSH gives a very different picture of a bishop—one dispassionately observed in a Bellini painting:

> *How came this bishop here in the elaborate fish-scales*
> *Of his gold surplice, weighed down, unable to run,*

*Unable to flee anywhere in the precise*
*Enclosing landscape, across the fields to the town*
*Or into the formality of the far pink hills?*

Another form of the portrait poem is found in THE NEGRO BOY
by David Samwell (1751–1798), of Nantglyn, Denbighshire, who
wrote in both languages. A parson's son, he became surgeon on
Captain Cook's ship "Discovery" and was an eye-witness of
the explorer's death. THE NEGRO BOY is a poem which, under the
device of portraying an African princeling—who "having been
asked what he gave for his Watch? answered, What I will never
give again: I gave a fine Boy for it", makes a sharp social comment:

> *In Isles that deck the western wave,*
> *I doom'd the hapless youth to dwell;*
> *A poor, forlorn, insulted slave!*
> *A beast—that Christians buy and sell!*
> *And in their cruel tasks employ*
> *The much enduring Negro Boy.*

On a much more sustained scale, Glyn Jones's THE DREAM OF
JAKE HOPKINS uses portraiture to make a critical comment
(intensified by contrast with the moving and lyrical portrait of
the grandmother) on the school system in Wales; and R. S.
Thomas's long poem THE MINISTER uses portraiture to comment
on rural Welsh Nonconformity.

Other portrait poems in contemporary Anglo-Welsh Literature
which frame clear pictures are Roland Mathias's A LETTER,
Leslie Norris's SIENCYN AP NICOLAS UPON HIS DEATH BED,
Robert Morgan's THE CARPENTER, Meic Stephen's THE JUNIOR
MASTER, John Idris Jones's TO IOAN MADOG, POET, ANCESTOR,
and the portrait poems of John Ormond.

# XV

The best thing in POEMS BY HUGHES, a volume which has already
been mentioned, is a sequence of light verses written in January
1839 in the form of a correspondence between T. Hughes and
Richard Newcome, archdeacon of Merioneth, warden of
Ruthin. Hughes begins it:

> *Here's a good piece of Cheese, (I perhaps might have kept it)*
> *But I hope the Archdeacon will kindly accept it,*
> *Nor suppose I deem wanting, in bara a chaws—*
> *A chroesaw—the Cloisters—a liberal house.*
> *To remain in my larder it's rather too nice,*
> *For a part has already been eaten by mice . . .*
> *These poor silly lines, Sir, I beg you'll excuse,*
> *And accept the respects of your Curate. T. Hughes.*

To this the archdeacon replies:

> *I should deem it, dear Curate, believe me, a crime,*
> *Did I fail in an instant reply to your rhyme . . .*
> *I trust that your present will act as a charm*
> *On Meirion's people—for there from each farm*
> *I've a claim (but in vain) of an annual cheese,*
> *But they hurl me defiance, and dare me to seize;*
> *Whilst you, haelionus-ddyn! tho' but a Curate,*
> *Who's stipend's not better than would be the poor-rate,*
> *Have proved by your gift that you're willing, as able,*
> *To supply to your Warden the wants of his table—*
> *For ('tis truth that I tell!) to my sorrow I find*
> *All the cheese in my house is eat down to the rind . . .*
> *Excuse, my dear sir, this attempt at recording*
> *My thanks. I remain, your affectionate Warden.*

The verse correspondence is closed with THE REJOINDER:

*Tho' farmers of Meirion the claims do defy*
*Of the Bishop's right hand, and the Bishop's right eye,*
*Yet deplore not your loss, for a cheese made in Meirion,*
*Will mostly turn out what is called cosyn gwirion;*
*Except where Sir Robert of Nannau has built on*
*His grange a good dairy producing Mock Stilton . . .*
*My regards at the Cloisters, to all, and to each,*
*And believe me, dear sir, your respectful—T.H.*

These verses are interesting, in contrast with the rest of POEMS BY HUGHES, in that the assumption that they are not poetry has liberated the writer from his habitual platitudinous solemnities and conventional diction, enabling him to exploit his obtrusive rhymes and to arrive at a colloquial line which exactly captures the formal facetiousness of these exchanges between two nineteenth century Welsh clerical gentlemen.

Another style of light verse is found in the LYRICS AND PHILLIPICS (1859) of Sir John Scourfield (1808–1876)—born Phillips, at Williamston, Pembrokeshire. Here is a stanza from his JOHN BRIGHT (whose name a north Wales secondary school bears to this day):

*The sun is said to rule the Day,*
*And the Moon to rule the Night,*
*But so unevenly—that they*
*Should both be ruled by Bright.*
*They're quite disorderly, and wrong,*
*And very badly taught,*
*And now, some Days, and Nights, are long,*
*And some of them are short.*
*For there's but one Man to Command,*
*One Man who's always right,*
*There is but one Man in the Land,*
*And that's myself—John Bright.*

If Lewis Morris's THE FISHING LASS OF HAKIN contains elements of parody, this also forms a part of the light verse of such twentieth century Anglo-Welsh practitioners as A. G. Prys-Jones and Dylan Thomas. The Revd. Eli Jenkins's morning hymn in UNDER MILK WOOD is to some extent a parody of an earlier Anglo-Welsh poem, W. H. Davies's DAYS THAT HAVE BEEN, with its easy topographical nostalgia:

> *Can I forget the banks of Malpas Brook,*
> *Or Ebbw's voice in such a wild delight,*
> *As on he dashed with pebbles in his throat,*
> *Gurgling towards the sea with all his might?*

But Dylan Thomas's verses do not parody the form of W. H. Davies's decasyllabics. The UNDER MILK WOOD morning hymn has a distinctive form of alternating lines of eight and seven syllables, with more often than not a feminine rhyme:

> *By Cerreg Cennen, King of time,*
> *Our Heron Head is only*
> *A bit of stone with seaweed spread*
> *Where gulls come to be lonely.*

Exactly the same form is found in the EMYN of Gwilym Marles (1834–1879), the bardic name of William Thomas, a Unitarian minister from north Carmarthenshire:

> *Ar daith y byd, ai byr ai hir,*
> *Duw, boed dy wir i'm tywys;*
> *Fy nef ddaearol ar bob cam*
> *Fo meddwl am dy 'wyllys.*

Gwilym Marles was the great-uncle of Dylan Thomas, whose middle name—Marlais—appears to commemorate the relationship. It is difficult to believe that the Anglo-Welsh poet, son of Welsh-speaking parents, spending his holidays in Carmarthenshire, had not at some time seen the slim volume—so redolent of its period—of the published writings of the Welsh poet among

68

his forefathers, and parodied some of his forms. The Revd. Eli Jenkins's evening hymn is in a different metre from the morning effusion:

> *We are not wholly bad or good*
> *Who live our lives under Milk Wood,*
> *And Thou, I know, wilt be the first*
> *To see our best side, not our worst;*

but this too is found in the ANERCHIAD PRIODASOL of Gwilym Marles:

> *O gylch eich traed yn ddiddan blaid*
> *Plant tyner chwariont yn ddi baid,*
> *Nes teimloch pan ar fynd i'r ne'*
> *Y cwyd eich plant i lanw eich lle.*

In A LITTLE NONSENSE (1954) A. G. Prys-Jones parodies various Anglo-Welsh, English and American writers, and deploys his technical skill in the craft of poetry to comment delicately on aspects of Welsh life—using notably the clerihew and the limerick, as in

> *There was a young man of Porthcawl*
> *Who thought he was Samson or Saul:*
> *These thoughts so obscure*
> *Were due to the brewer,*
> *And not to his ego at all.*

The most successful contemporary Anglo-Welsh satire in verse is that of Harri Webb. A highly accomplished example is his CYWYDD O FAWL, which satirizes the *cywydd* form, the poem of praise, the diction of Caradoc Evans, the alleged characteristics of the inhabitants of Cardiganshire, and also those of the Welsh Arts Council.

# XVI

The nineteenth century adds to the earlier example of Huw ap
Huw (1693–1776), Y Bardd Coch o Fôn, further instances of the
phenomenon of a Welsh poet attempting Anglo-Welsh poetry.
To write worthwhile poetry in both languages is a rare achievement—Morgan Llwyd and Lewis Morris o Fôn are the exceptions.

Islwyn (William Thomas, 1832–1878) is not, and his ENGLISH
POEMS—published posthumously in 1913—are of little interest. The
same is true of Talhaiarn (John Jones, 1810–1869). Another who
made the attempt was the Archdruid Gwili (John Jenkins,
1872–1936)—born at Pontardulais, Carmarthenshire, and educated
at University College, Cardiff, and Jesus College, Oxford. His
POEMS (1920) are undistinguished, though one—EDWARD
EASTAWAY—is of some interest in that it is the pseudonym of
Edward Thomas. The poem, which recalls their joint exploration
of the Carmarthenshire countryside during Oxford vacations
(Thomas read history under Owen M. Edwards), also reminds us
of the strength of Edward Thomas's attachment to Wales, where
his parents were born. Other evidence of this is his edition of THE
POEMS OF JOHN DYER in 1903 (for O. M. Edwards's "Welsh
Library" series), and his volume of CELTIC STORIES (1922) for
children, four of which are from the MABINOGI. It was largely
through the good offices of Edward Thomas that the early work of
another Anglo-Welsh poet, W. H. Davies, received recognition.
Yet another Anglo-Welsh poet, R. S. Thomas, has edited a
SELECTED POEMS OF EDWARD THOMAS.

It has become the fashion to mock at the achievement of Sir
Lewis Morris (1833–1907)—born in Carmarthen, and educated at
Jesus College, Oxford. The poetic conventions of his day—
prolixity, romanticism-and-water—almost swamp his talent, but
he was not of the family of Lewis Morris o Fôn for nothing. Exact
observation is to be seen in some of the stanzas of LYDSTEP

CAVERNS, where the green calm of rock-pools after a storm is evoked, and the "creaming filmy shallows creep". His poem ST DAVID'S HEAD shows a remarkable awareness of the sense not only of huge but of sinister antiquity to be felt in Dewisland—so much at variance with its later and more easily evoked associations:

> *Think of the numberless far-away centuries, long before man,*
> *When the hot earth with monsters teemed, and with monsters*
> > *the deep,*
> *And the red sun loomed faint, and the moon was caught fast in*
> > *the motionless air,*
> *And the warm waves seethed through the haze in a secular*
> > *sleep.*
> > *Rock was here and headland then,*
> > *Ere the little lives of men.*

> *Over it long the mastodons crashed through the tropical forest,*
> *And the great bats swooped overhead through the half-defined*
> > *blue;*
> *Then they passed, and the hideous ape-man, speechless and*
> > *half-erect,*
> *Through weary ages of time tore and gibbered and slew.*
> > *Grayer skies and chiller air,*
> > *But the self-same rock was there.*

Eben Jones (1820–1860) was born of a London Welsh family, of austerely Calvinist tendency, which returned to Wales upon the wreck of its fortunes. This event projected the sons into the necessity of supporting themselves, and thus into the world of contemporary ideas. Eben Jones—who had the attractive trait from boyhood of "a decided and not a mere theoretical leaning to a Republican form of Government"—at the age of nineteen contributed to Robert Owen's NEW MORAL WORLD, and became a disciple of Owen. By the time he was thirty he "would hardly talk on any subject but Chartism"—according to Dante Gabriel Rossetti, who in 1870 answered a question on him in NOTES AND QUERIES. The aim of this intense, committed, and highly individual young man was to be a "poetical thinker", and in his eighteenth year he wrote an ODE TO THOUGHT which has an urgency of movement and a vigour of imagery which make it a memorable achievement at that age. His STUDIES OF SENSATION AND EVENT (1843–1879) contain several poems in which an individual and authentic voice is to be heard. Perhaps the best of them is the sonnet HIGH SUMMER, with its technical skill, its seeking after an exact diction, and its sensuous—almost voluptuous—evocation of complete physical relaxation:

> *I never wholly feel that summer is high,*
> *However green the trees, or loud the birds,*
> *However movelessly eye-winking herds*
> *Stand in field ponds, or under large trees lie,*
> *Till I do climb all cultured pastures by,*
> *That hedged by hedgerows studiously fretted trim,*
> *Smile like a lady's face with lace laced prim,*
> *And on some moor or hill that seeks the sky*
> *Lonely and nakedly,—utterly lie down,*
> *And feel the sunshine throbbing on body and limb,*
> *My drowsy brain in pleasant drunkenness swim,*
> *Each rising thought sink back and dreamily drown,*
> *Smiles creep o'er my face, and smother my lips, and cloy,*
> *Each muscle sink to itself, and separately enjoy.*

This is a poem that sends one to Idris Davies's treatment of the same theme in HIGH SUMMER ON THE MOUNTAINS, to Leslie Norris's superb evocation of a hot summer's day in his poem WATER, and to John Stuart Williams's ANOTHER ISLAND IN THE SUN, where

> *The sun sings like*
> *a guitar struck with an open hand.*

# XVII

In an interesting and informative article, Mr. Gerald Morgan has noted that the roots of Anglo-Welsh fiction are to be sought in the eighteenth century, and he suggests that the first Anglo-Welsh novel may be THE ADVENTURES AND VAGARIES OF TWM SHON CATTI (1828) by Thomas Jeffery Llewelyn Prichard. At all events, its publication marks the appearance of the literary form which is to be a major preoccupation of Anglo-Welsh Literature in the twentieth century—so much so that in 1938 it seemed to Mr. Saunders Lewis that Anglo-Welsh writers were "mostly novelists". In a more specific sense, it represents an interest in Welsh history as material for the novel, parallel to the interest in it we have seen in poetry, which is to reach a major statement in the OWEN GLENDOWER (1940) of John Cowper Powys. What might be called the Nonconformist novel—which in its most creative form is to be found in some of the novels of Emyr Humphreys—is perhaps first represented in Margam Jones's THE STARS OF THE REVIVAL (1909). This strange but at moments quite powerful novel so patently touches the world of Caradoc Evans's writings that one wonders whether he may not have read it. Certainly it is part of the world upon which Harri Webb's poem SYNOPSIS OF THE GREAT WELSH NOVEL makes a hilarious and astringent comment.

As we have seen, Anglo-Welsh prose—as distinct from Anglo-Welsh prose-fiction—has its origins in the sixteenth century. The exact nature of its dimensions is difficult to judge since so little work has yet been done in this field, but they are likely to prove extensive. Among notable letter-writers, for example, there is James Howell; many of the letters of Evan Evans, the Morris brothers, Goronwy Owen, are in English; Professor Price quotes Evan Lloyd on letter-writing—"an easy flowing deshabille for a Letter I say—a Nightgown and Slippers are the only dress to write one in", and tells us that his letters combine this informality with an elegance that gives them distinction.

Edward Herbert of Cherbury's early broaching of autobiography as a prose form is sustained in THE LIFE OF ROBERT OWEN BY HIMSELF (1857), and in the REMINISCENCES OF CAPTAIN GRONOW (1862) by the Swansea-born Rees Howell Gronow, who was present at Waterloo. In the twentieth century the form is continued in W. H. Davies's AUTOBIOGRAPHY OF A SUPER-TRAMP (1908); the autobiographical writings of Arthur Machen—FAR OFF THINGS (1922) and THINGS NEAR AND FAR (1923); Sir Henry Jones's OLD MEMORIES (1923); the AUTOBIOGRAPHY (1934) of John Cowper Powys; Wyn Griffith's SPRING OF YOUTH (1935); the autobiographical writings of Jack Jones—UNFINISHED JOURNEY (1937), ME AND MINE (1946), GIVE ME BACK MY HEART (1950); Augustus John's CHIAROSCURO (1952), and various more recent volumes by other writers. It is a noteworthy and prolific Anglo-Welsh prose genre—and is perhaps another manifestation of that preoccupation with the past, and alleged tendency to nostalgia, which characterize Anglo-Welsh poetry.

In 1938 the historical prose of Sir John Edward Lloyd, T. P. Ellis, A. W. Wade-Evans, seemed to Mr. Saunders Lewis to be among the most significant and committed Anglo-Welsh writing. Again, a line of antiquarian and topographical writing descends from George Owen of Henllys (1552–1613)—through Thomas Pennant and a number of others, to be continued in our own day by Cledwyn Hughes.

The publication of the first number of THE WELSH REVIEW in 1892, and of O. M. Edwards's WALES in 1894, are indicative of the massive shift that was occurring in the language situation as a consequence of the industrial revolution and compulsory English-language education (to be re-inforced in the twentieth century by such factors as compulsory military service, the decline of Welsh Nonconformity, the very extensive use of English in higher education, and the revolutions in transport and communications, which have reversed the balance of the languages of Wales). Bilingual and English-language periodicals were now viable. A second WELSH REVIEW (1906) and the long-lived WELSH OUT-

LOOK, together with a number of other magazines, were to intervene before the establishment of Keidrych Rhys's WALES in 1937, and Gwyn Jones's WELSH REVIEW in 1939. In 1949 what is now THE ANGLO-WELSH REVIEW was founded, to be joined in 1965 by POETRY WALES, MABON (1969), and PLANET (1970). The part played by this sequence of Anglo-Welsh periodicals—in the stimulation of the short-story, of poetry, of critical writing, and of a growing sense of cohesion and literary tradition—cannot be over-estimated. This essay has drawn heavily upon them, as any Anglo-Welsh studies are bound to do.

In the last decades of the nineteenth century the first generation of twentieth century Anglo-Welsh writers was being born—W. H. Davies (1871–1940), John Cowper Powys (1872–1963), Edward Thomas (1878–1917), Jack Jones (1884–1970), Huw Menai (1887–1961), Wyn Griffith (b. 1890), David Jones (b. 1895), and A. G. Prys-Jones (b. 1888)—whose anthology WELSH POETS (1917) was the first of a line. This was resumed in Keidrych Rhys's MODERN WELSH POETRY (1944), continued in Gwyn Williams's PRESENTING WELSH POETRY (1959), sustained in Bryn Griffiths' WELSH VOICES (1967), and completed in Gerald Morgan's THIS WORLD OF WALES (1968) and THE LILTING HOUSE edited in 1969 by John Stuart Williams and Meic Stephens. To much of all this, Glyn Jones's THE DRAGON HAS TWO TONGUES (1968) is an indispensable handbook, as is A BIBLIOGRAPHY OF ANGLO-WELSH LITERATURE 1900–1965 by Brynmor Jones, published in 1970.

The prose link with the nineteenth century is completed by Caradoc Evans (1883–1945)—the publication of whose volume MY PEOPLE in 1915 is taken by some, a little arbitrarily, to mark the beginning of Anglo-Welsh Literature.

# XVIII

Pointing out that our view of the Greece of the fifth century B.C. is in fact a partial, Athenian view, Professor E. H. Carr (at one time holder of the chair of International Politics at Aberystwyth) has made this comment: "Our picture has been preselected and predetermined for us, not so much by accident as by people who were consciously or unconsciously imbued with a particular view and thought the facts which supported that view worth preserving". He goes on to quote Professor G. Barraclough's dictum that "The history we read, though based on facts, is, strictly speaking, not factual at all, but a series of accepted judgments". In the belief that these points of view can shed a certain light upon literary history too, I should like to conclude by applying them to a selection of statements about Anglo-Welsh Literature, and examine the consequences.

Typical accepted judgments about Anglo-Welsh Literature, with the date of their appearance, are the following: "Anglo-Welsh writing . . . is a child almost of our own times" (1951); "The Anglo-Welsh have . . . no long tradition of speaking English while remaining Welsh" (1952); "The Anglo-Welsh had to import and adapt their culture from an uninteresting and im-poverished England during a period of unhealthy flux which is not yet over" (1953); "There is no continuity of tradition that can be described as an Anglo-Welsh literary stream until we reach the present century" (1953); "(The) present world began just forty years ago, with the publication of MY PEOPLE in 1915" (1957); "Caradoc Evans is the father of Anglo-Welsh Literature" (1964).

The first of these statements was made by myself in an editorial of the Anglo-Welsh review then called DOCK LEAVES, and if I had been asked upon what evidence I founded it I suppose I should have said that everybody knew that only a handful of Welshmen had written poetry in English until our own time. This

76

was substantially the argument of the article entitled WALES AND THE ANGLO-WELSH, by Mr. Ioan Bowen Rees, from which the second quotation is taken (an article to which I have referred in section VI of this essay). With four departments of English flourishing in the University of Wales, I assumed (as a recent graduate of one of them) that any evidence of an opposite tendency—of a considerable number of Welshmen of earlier times writing poetry or prose in English, but out of the experience of being Welsh—would have been uncovered long since.

Nonetheless, Mr. Ioan Bowen Rees's position—though it was also my own—seemed to depend upon too many unproved assumptions. To satisfy myself, and to construct as fully documented an argument as possible (which was of some importance to my predicament then as the young editor of the only Anglo-Welsh periodical in existence), I decided to establish as conclusively as I could that such evidence as there was led inevitably to the accepted judgments.

I planned my proof along two lines of argument. Deductively I would show that the English language was of such recent provenance in Wales that its creative use by Welshmen was more or less a twentieth century phenomenon: and thus that an Anglo-Welsh Literature could not yet exist. Inductively I would demonstrate that, before the present century, only a handful of writers—of dubious Welshness—had in fact produced poetry and prose in English: and thus that an Anglo-Welsh Literature did not yet exist.

A very little work along these two approaches—on the one hand the investigation of the history of English as a language of Wales, and on the other the investigation of how many Welshmen had in fact published poetry or prose in English—led me almost immediately to suspect that the conclusions which would eventually be forthcoming would be directly opposed to those I had hoped to demonstrate. My original intention had been to file every reference I could find to a Welsh writer who had published anything in English. In a short time I discovered that the volume of recording this involved was quite beyond my limitations, and I restricted my work to poetry published in English. The present essay consists of an outline of material that has come to light in this way over the last sixteen years. It has been compiled without benefit of library, or research procedures; it has been taken from secondary, printed sources; the work has had to be done in the midst of the family circle, in our various homes in Wales and the Netherlands. I could have wished that the poets might have been served with scholarship, instead of merely with affection.

The interesting question remains why the accepted judgments were—and, for all I know, still are—accepted. To return to the quotation from Professor Carr, what were the factors that "preselected and predetermined" the picture for us? What was the "particular view" with which the contemporary commentators were "consciously or unconsciously imbued" when they formulated or repeated these judgments? These are questions of some interest, for they imply an interpretation of reality with which it is desired that the evidence shall conform. That interpretation, I suspect, is what might be called the Athenian view of Wales. I am inclined to think that most of the accepted judgments I have quoted are not really literary judgments at all. Though they appear to be concerned with Anglo-Welsh Literature, they are in fact concerned—consciously or unconsciously—with something quite different.

The context in which my own accepted judgment, quoted at the beginning of the second paragraph of this section, was uttered may shed some light upon the others. It appeared in the editorial of DOCK LEAVES (as it then was) for Michaelmas 1951. What called it forth, I find, was a remark in a speech by a south Wales Member of Parliament of that time. "The soul of Wales", he had said, "is finding expression in the Anglo-Welsh school of poets and authors." These were the days of the Home Rule petition and the Welsh Rule at the Eisteddfod, and the Anglo-

Welsh were being used as a stick with which to beat them both. The mawkish formulation of the Parliamentarian's opinion, and my own adherence to the objects at which it was directed, preselected and predetermined my own judgment. Such facts as I knew of appeared to confirm, as it was desirable they should, the view of Wales which I held—and it was this, and not Anglo-Welsh Literature, with which my judgment was concerned.

I should like, therefore, to conclude with three suggestions. The first is that judgments upon Anglo-Welsh Literature have often been not literary judgments at all but sociological ones. The perpetuation of accepted judgments without reference to a body of evidence unfavourable to them—and their use in support of positions quite other than those to which the judgments seem to relate—can only generate heat, not light: no cause, however admirable, can be advanced in this way. The Athenian view of Wales—by which I mean the view that sees the Welsh language and its culture as the acropolis of most that is best in the past and present of Wales—does not in the least depend upon the denigration of Anglo-Welsh Literature, open or implied. Nor, it may be added, is the status of English Literature in any way dependent upon such tactics.

I have written elsewhere of my conviction that in a bilingual situation, whether in education or in society at large, what is to be avoided above all is a rivalry between the languages and cultures. No one can foretell what the disastrous failure in this respect may yet mean for Belgium, for Canada: perhaps the disintegration of the State. The whole aim of a bilingual education and a bilingual society must be to present the two languages and cultures as complementary. My second suggestion is that this is the social and educational function of Anglo-Welsh Literature in contemporary Wales.

My third suggestion is that some literary pleasure is to be got from these writers of the centuries before our own, "minute objects in the landscape" though (in Eliot's words) some of them may be.

79

At least I have found it so: over the last sixteen years they are the writers I have come to know best, and even from the very bad ones—Anne Penny, Ann of Swansea—I have got pleasure and, as one concerned with the practice of writing today, learned much that is valuable. I hope that some others may discover this, and that among them may be some of the Anglo-Welsh writers of our own time. Because this slight study of its past has illuminated and enriched my understanding of the Anglo-Welsh Literature of the present, and thus of Wales today, I should like to think of this essay as having been written in some sense in honour of four writers with whom I have had varying degrees of acquaintance: Idris Davies, Vernon Watkins, Dylan Thomas, and John Cowper Powys.

*We die with the dying:*
*See, they depart, and we go with them.*
*We are born with the dead:*
*See, they return, and bring us with them.*

# XIX

Brief biographical and bibliographical details of some Anglo-Welsh poets—from the fifteenth to the twentieth century—are listed below and on the pages that follow. There is little doubt that this landscape contains considerably more "minute objects" than are recorded here. The main sources are Y BYWGRAFFIADUR CYMREIG HYD 1940; THE DICTIONARY OF NATIONAL BIOGRAPHY; A BIOGRAPHICAL DICTIONARY OF EMINENT WELSHMEN (Revd. Robert Williams, Llandovery, 1852); EMINENT WELSHMEN (Asaph, 1908); ENWOGION CYMREIG, 1700–1900 (Parch. T. Morgan, Sciwen, 1907); and the writings of the poets themselves. Acknowledgements to individuals are made in section XX.

IEUAN AP HYWEL SWRDWAL (fl. 1430–1480)
associated with Newtown and Machynlleth, Montgomeryshire. Bilingual. HYMN TO THE VIRGIN, c. 1470 (restored text printed in The Transactions of the Honourable Society of Cymmrodorion, Session 1954).

MORRIS KYFFIN (c. 1555–1598)
b. Oswestry. Bilingual. THE BLESSEDNES OF BRYTAINE, 1587 (reprinted for the Hon. Soc. of Cymmrodorion, 1885).

RICHARD WILIAM (fl. 1590–1630)
Priest of a parish in east Glamorgan. "Syr Risiart y Fwyalchen" (Sir Richard the Blackbird). Bilingual. SIR RICHARD'S CONFESSION (given in HEN GWNDIDAU, CAROLAU A CHYWYDDAU, ed. Hopcyn and Cadrawd, Bangor, 1910).

Sir JOHN STRADLING (1563–1637)
b. St. Donat's? Educ. Oxford. BEATI PACIFICI, 1623. DIVINE POEMS, 1625.

JOHN DAVIES (c. 1565–1618)
Writing-master. b. Hereford. Bilingual, called "The Welsh Poet". THE COMPLETE WORKS OF JOHN DAVIES OF HEREFORD (Two volumes, Chertsey Worthies Library, 1878). Article in THE ANGLO-WELSH REVIEW No. 28 by Father H. E. G. Rope.

HUGH HOLLAND (1569–1633)
b. Denbigh. Educ. Westminster & Cambridge. Bilingual? VERSES IN DESCRIPTION OF THE CHIEF CITIES OF EUROPE. A CYPRES GARLAND, 1625. (Two essays on him published as HUGH HOLLAND, Gwasg y Brython, 1943.)

Sir WILLIAM VAUGHAN (1577–1641)
b. Gelli, Aur, Carms. Educ. Jesus College, Oxford. THE CHURCH MILITANT, 1640.

EDWARD, Lord HERBERT of Cherbury (1583–1648)
b. Eyton-on-Severn. Educ. Oxford. THE AUTOBIOGRAPHY OF EDWARD LORD HERBERT OF CHERBURY (Nimmo, 1886).

GEORGE HERBERT (1593–1633)
Anglican parson. b. Montgomery Castle. Educ. Westminster & Cambridge. THE TEMPLE, 1633.

ROWLAND WATKYNS (d. 1664)
Anglican parson. b. Longtown, Hereford. FLAMMA SINE FUMO, 1662 (ed. Paul C. Davies, University of Wales Press, 1968). Article in THE ANGLO-WELSH REVIEW No. 38 by Paul Davies.

JAMES HOWELL (c. 1594–1666)
Historiographer-royal. b. Cefnbryn, Brecon. Educ. Jesus College, Oxford. Bilingual. POEMS UPON DIVERS EMERGENT OCCASIONS, 1664. Article "James Howell in Spain" in DOCK LEAVES Winter 1956, by Gareth Alban Davies.

DAVID LLOYD (1597–1663)
Dean of St Asaph. b. Llanidloes. Educ. Oxford. Bilingual. THE
LEGEND OF CAPTAIN JONES, 1631.

Sir ROGER LORTE (1608–1664)
b. Stackpole, Pembs. Educ. Oxford. "He was considered a good
English poet, and about 1647 he published a volume of poems."

MORGAN LLWYD (1619–1659)
b. Maentwrog, Merioneth. Educ. Wrexham. Bilingual. GWEITH-
IAU MORGAN LLWYD O WYNEDD (ed. Thomas Ellis, Bangor &
London, 1899) gives 52 poems of which 31 are in English, together
with some English prose.

HENRY VAUGHAN (1621–1695)
the Silurist. Physician. b. Trenewydd, Brecon. Educ. Jesus
College, Oxford. Bilingual. SILEX SCINTILLANS, 1650, etc.

THOMAS VAUGHAN (1621-1695)
Anglican parson, twin brother of the above. Educ. Jesus College,
Oxford. Bilingual. Poetry in Welsh, English and Latin. Article
on him in THE ANGLO-WELSH REVIEW No. 42 by Eluned
Crawshaw.

WILLIAM WILLIAMS (fl. 1648–1677)
b. Cardiganshire? POETICAL PIETY; or POETRY MADE PIOUS, 1677.

GEORGE STEPNEY (1663–1707)
Diplomat. b. Prendergast, Pembs. Educ. Westminster & Cambridge. Poems published in THE WORKS OF THE MINOR POETS,
1749. Contributed to Dryden's MISCELLANY POEMS. Article on
him in Johnson's LIVES OF THE POETS.

DAVID LEWIS (c. 1683–1760)
b. Llanddewi Efelffre, Pembs. Educ. Jesus College, Oxford. Four
volumes of poetry in English between 1726 and 1732.

JANE BRERETON (1685–1740)
b. Mold, Flint. POEMS ON SEVERAL OCCASIONS published posthumously in 1744.

HUGH HUGHES (1693–1776)
"Huw ap Huw" or "Y Bardd Coch o Fôn". b. Llandyfrydog, Anglesey. Bilingual. "He became a good Welsh scholar, and wrote several poems in Welsh and English."

JOHN DYER (1699–1757)
Painter, later an Anglican parson. b. Aberglasni, Carms., son of a solicitor. Educ. Westminster. GRONGAR HILL, 1727. THE POEMS OF JOHN DYER ed. Edward Thomas (The Welsh Library, Fisher Unwin, 1903).

LEWIS MORRIS (1701–1765)
"Llewelyn Ddu o Fôn". b. Llanfihangel Tre'r Beirdd, Anglesey. Educ. Beaumaris. Bilingual. Poetry in both languages.

ANNA WILLIAMS (1706–1783)
b. Rosemarket, Pembs. MISCELLANIES IN PROSE AND VERSE, 1766.

Sir CHARLES HANBURY WILLIAMS (1708–1759)
b. Pont-y-Pwl. Educ. Eton. WORKS in three volumes, 1822.

WILLIAM WILLIAMS (1717–1791)
"Pantycelyn". b. Cefncoed, Carms, Bilingual. HOSANNA TO THE SON OF DAVID, 1759.

EDWARD DAVIES (1718–1789)
Anglican parson. b. Monmouthshire? BLAISE CASTLE, 1783. CHEPSTOW: A POEM, 1784 (reprinted 1952).

PETER WILLIAMS (1723–1796)
Methodist minister. b. Llansadyrnin, Carms. Bilingual. HYMNS ON VARIOUS SUBJECTS, 1771.

84

ANNE PENNY (fl. 1729–1780)
b. Bangor? Published four collections of poems between 1762 and 1780.

EVAN EVANS (1731–1788)
"Ieuan Fardd" or "Ieuan Brydydd Hir". Anglican parson. b. Lledrod, Cards. Educ. Ystrad Meurig and Oxford. Bilingual. THE LOVE OF OUR COUNTRY, 1772 and several other poems in English. (Discussed in Chapter VI of A SCHOOL OF WELSH AUGUSTANS by Saunders Lewis, reprinted 1969.)

EVAN LLOYD (1734–1776)
Anglican parson. b. Bala, Merioneth, son of an impoverished squire. Educ. Ruthin & Jesus College, Oxford. Four long poems published between 1766 and 1768: THE POWERS OF THE PEN, THE CURATE, THE METHODIST, CONVERSATION. (Lecture "a Man of Genius, and a Welsh Man" by Professor Cecil J. L. Price: University College, Swansea, 1963.)

RICHARD FENTON (1747–1821)
b. St David's, Pembs. Educ. Oxford. POEMS, 1773. POEMS, 1790.

EDWARD WILLIAMS (1747–1826)
"Iolo Morganwg". b. Llancarfan. Bilingual. POEMS LYRIC AND PASTORAL, 1794.

CHARLES SYMMONS (1749–1826)
Anglican parson. b. Cardigan. Educ. Westminster, Univ. of Glasgow, Cambridge. INEZ, 1797. CONSTANTIA, 1800.

DAVID SAMWELL (1751–1798)
Surgeon on the "Discovery". b. Nantyglyn, Denbigh, son of the vicar. Bilingual. Poetry in both languages. Article "David Samwell; A Further Note" by W. Llewelyn Davies, in Transactions of the Hon. Soc. of Cymmrodorion, Session 1938, gives text of poem THE NEGRO BOY.

RICHARD LLWYD (1752–1835)
"The Bard of Snowdon". b. Beaumaris. Bilingual. BEAUMARIS
BAY, 1800. GAYTON WAKE, 1804. POEMS, TALES, ODES, SONNETS,
TRANSLATIONS FROM THE BRITISH, 1804.

DAVID LLOYD (1752–1838)
Anglican parson. b. Llanbister, Radnor. THE VOYAGE OF LIFE,
1792.

ELIEZER WILLIAMS (1754–1820)
Anglican parson. b. Carmarthen. Educ. Queen Eliz. Grammar
School & Jesus College, Oxford. NAUTICAL ODES, OR POETICAL
SKETCHES, DESIGNED TO COMMEMORATE THE ACHIEVEMENTS OF
THE BRITISH NAVY, 1801.

EDWARD DAVIES (1756–1831)
Anglican parson. b. Llanfaredd, Radnor. Educ. Brecon School.
APHTHARTE, THE GENIUS OF BRITAIN, 1784.

JOHN WALTERS (1760–1789)
b. Llandochau, Glam. Educ. Jesus College, Oxford. Bilingual.
POEMS, WITH NOTES, 1780.

JOHN THELWALL (1764–1834)
b. London of the family of Plas-y-ward, Denbigh, and farmed in
Brecon at one stage. POEMS UPON VARIOUS SUBJECTS, 1787. POEMS
WRITTEN IN CLOSE CONFINEMENT IN THE TOWER AND NEWGATE,
1795. POEMS CHIEFLY WRITTEN IN RETIREMENT . . . WITH A PREFA-
TORY MEMOIR OF THE LIFE OF THE AUTHOR, 1801.

JULIA ANN HATTON (1764–1838)
"Ann of Swansea". b. Worcester, a sister of Mrs. Siddons. POEMS
ON MISCELLANEOUS SUBJECTS, 1783. POETIC TRIFLES, 1811.

DAVID HUGHES (fl. 1770–1817)
Anglican parson, headmaster of Ruthin School. b. Denbighshire?
Bilingual. POEMS BY HUGHES published posthumously in 1865.

TALIESIN WILLIAMS (1787–1847)
"Taliesin ab Iolo". b. Cardiff. Bilingual. CARDIFF CASTLE, 1827.
THE DOOM OF COLYN DOLPHYN, 1837.

JOHN JONES (1788–1858)
"Poet Jones". b. Llanasa, Flint. Bilingual. THE COTTON MILL,
1821. THE SOVEREIGN, 1827. POEMS BY JOHN JONES, 1856.

THOMAS MARSDEN (1802–1849)
Anglican parson. b. Lampeter. Educ. St David's College. Bilingual.
THE POET'S ORCHARD, 1848.

JANE WILLIAMS (1806–1885)
b. London of Welsh family, she learnt Welsh and studied Welsh
Literature. MISCELLANEOUS POEMS, 1824.

Sir JOHN SCOURFIELD, born PHILLIPS (1808-1876)
b. Williamston, Pembs. Educ. Harrow and Oxford. LYRICS AND
PHILLIPICS, 1859.

JOHN JONES (1810–1869)
"Talhaiarn". Architect. b. Llanfairtalhaearn, Denbs. GWAITH
TALHAIARN in 3 volumes, 1855, 1862, 1869. Bilingual. Poetry in
both languages.

GEORGE BAXTER (1815–1854)
b. Llanllwch-haiarn, Montgomery. DON JUAN JUNIOR; A POEM BY
BYRON'S GHOST, 1839.

RICHARD HALL (1817–1866)
Shopkeeper. b. Brecon. A TALE OF THE PAST AND OTHER POEMS,
1850.

T. HUGHES (fl. 1818–1865)
Anglican parson. b. Ruthin? son of David Hughes (see above).
Educ. Bangor. Bilingual. Published POEMS FROM HUGHES, 1865,
consisting of his father's and his own poems in Welsh, Latin and
English.

EBEN JONES (1820–1860)
b. London of a Welsh family which returned to Wales. STUDIES
OF SENSATION AND EVENT, 1843, 1879.

THOMAS JEFFERY LLEWELYN PRICHARD (d. 1875)
Travelling actor. b. Trallong, Brecon. Bilingual. WELSH
MINSTRELSY, 1824. THE ADVENTURES AND VAGARIES OF TWM
SHON CATTI, Aberystwyth 1828. Article in THE ANGLO-WELSH
REVIEW No. 39 by Gerald Morgan.

TITUS LEWIS (1822–1887)
b. Llanelli. Bilingual. THE SOLDIER'S WIFE, A TALE OF INKERMAN,
1855.

ELLIS ROBERTS (1827–1895)
"Elis Wyn o Wyrfai". Anglican parson. b. Llandwrog, Caerns.
Bilingual. WRECK OF THE LONDON, 1865.

JOHN MORGAN (1827–1903)
Anglican parson. b. Trefdraeth, Pembs. Bilingual. MY WELSH
HOME, 1870.

WILLIAM THOMAS (1832–1878)
"Islwyn". Methodist minister. b. Ynys-ddu, Monmouth.
Bilingual. ISLWYN's ENGLISH POEMS, published posthumously 1913.

Sir LEWIS MORRIS (1833–1907)
b. Carmarthen. Educ. Queen Eliz. Grammar School & Jesus
College, Oxford. THE WORKS OF LEWIS MORRIS, 1891.

GEORGE POWELL (1842–1882)
b. Nanteos, Aberystwyth. POEMS BY MIOLNIR NANTEOS, 1860.
Article in THE ANGLO-WELSH REVIEW No. 44 by David Lewis
Jones.

JOHN HUGHES (1850–1932)
b. Swansea. Bilingual. SONGS IN THE NIGHT, 1885. TRISTIORA, 1896.

ERNEST RHYS (1859–1946)
b. London of a Welsh family and spent his childhood in Carmarthen. WELSH BALLADS, 1898?

ELVET LEWIS (1860–1953)
"Elfed". Bilingual. b. Conwyl Elfed, Carms. Poetry in both languages.

W. H. DAVIES (1871–1940)
b. Newport, Mon. THE AUTOBIOGRAPHY OF A SUPER-TRAMP, 1908. COLLECTED POEMS, 1916.

JOHN JENKINS (1872–1936)
"Gwili". Theologian. b. Pontardulais, Carms. Educ. Univ. Coll. Cardiff and Jesus College, Oxford. Bilingual. ENGLISH POEMS, 1920.

JOHN COWPER POWYS (1872–1963)
b. Shirley, Derbyshire. Settled at Corwen 1934, Blaenau Ffestiniog 1955. Hon.D.Litt.(Wales). Autobiography, 1934. OWEN GLENDOWER, 1940. OBSTINATE CYMRIC, 1947. PORIUS, 1951. LETTERS, 1958. SELECTED POEMS published posthumously in 1964.

EDWARD THOMAS (1872–1917)
b. London of Welsh parents.

HUW MENAI (1887–1961)

IDRIS DAVIES (1905–1953)

VERNON WATKINS (1906–1967)

BRENDA CHAMBERLAIN (1912–1971)

DYLAN MARLAIS THOMAS (1914–1953)

ALUN LEWIS (1915–1944)

T. H. JONES (1921–1965)

# XX

Finally, to acknowledgements: and my first debt of gratitude is to Mr. Wyn Binding, head of the department of English and English Drama at Trinity College, Carmarthen, whose invitation to me to give an annual course of seminars in Anglo-Welsh Literature was responsible for the first shaping of material which had long lain dormant in dusty files. For their commission to write this short study, and thus give further shape to the material, I am grateful to the Literature Committee of the Welsh Arts Council, the University of Wales Press, and the joint editors of the WRITERS OF WALES series.

The first trial run of the earliest outline of this material was given in a paper to the Dock Leaves Group in perhaps 1953, and for their discussion and criticism of it—and particularly Roland Mathias's, then and thereafter—I have reason to be grateful. This apart, so little response did the material elicit in succeeding years, so firmly did all doors seem to be closed against further possibilities of exploration—let alone publication, that I gave up hope and was ready enough to accept—towards the end of 1960— an invitation to teach in the Netherlands. During my years there, the enthusiastic interest shown in this field by Mr. Gerald Morgan —communicated in letters and occasional meetings at the National Eisteddfod—began to revive my hope that there might after all be a role for Anglo-Welsh Literature in Wales today. For the enthusiasm and confidence of Mr. Morgan, which was the greatest source of encouragement to me then, I am extremely grateful.

That the moment at which one gives up hope is in fact the moment just before something is going to happen was abundantly demonstrated when, shortly after my return to Wales in 1967, the University of Wales Press published Mr. Morgan's Anglo-Welsh anthology THIS WORLD OF WALES—to be followed by the

## THE AUTHOR

Raymond Garlick was born in London in 1926, of wholly English family. He was educated at the University of Leeds, at University College, Bangor, and by the conversation over five years of John Cowper Powys. After teaching at various schools in Wales for twelve years, in 1961 he joined the staff of an International School in the Netherlands. He was appointed to a senior lectureship in the English Department at Trinity College, Carmarthen, in 1967, and four years later was made Director of Welsh Studies there.

He was a founder of THE ANGLO-WELSH REVIEW, which he edidet from 1949 to 1960. His Collected Poems, A SENSE OF EUROPE, were published by Gwasg Gomer in 1968 and received a Welsh Arts Council Prize. A further volume of poems, A SENSE OF TIME, appeared in 1972.

Davies-Dent publication of The Lilting House, edited by John Stuart Williams and Meic Stephens. Thus at last there appeared, within a year of each other, two books the need for which I had argued over a dozen years—before giving up in despair. Their publication, and the practical assistance given to this—and to the two literatures of Wales in many other ways—by the Welsh Arts Council, have been major sources of encouragement.

Among individual sources of help and advice, I must acknowledge with gratitude my colleague the Revd. Islwyn Jenkins, who introduced me to Sir Richard the Blackbird and to Margam Jones's novel; my colleagues Mr. Dafydd Rowlands and Mr. Carwyn James, who guided my stumbling steps in cynghanedd (and the latter also for putting me in touch with the writings of Gwilym Marles); Mr. John Davies, Librarian of Trinity College, Carmarthen; and Mr. G. A. Dickman of Haverfordwest, Mr. Ivor Waters of Chepstow, and Mr. R. T. Russell of Ruthin School, who were good enough to supply me with information about writers. I must also thank my students, against whose dialectic much of this material has been tried out, and whose response has often shed new light upon it for me.

Much of the first section formed part of a lecture given at the Taliesin Congress 1969, now published in Literature in Celtic Countries (1971) by the University of Wales Press. My debt to Professor David Williams's A History of Modern Wales (Murray, 1950) will be apparent at several points in sections II and III. These sections, and section IV, are also indebted to Professor Glanmor Williams's The Welsh Church from Conquest to Reformation (University of Wales Press, 1962). Other passages first appeared in the editorials of Dock Leaves, in an article entitled "Anglo-Welsh Poetry from 1587 to 1800" in the January-March 1954 number of The Dublin Magazine, and in the pages of The Welsh Anvil, Yr Athro, and Poetry Wales. Much of section XVIII appeared as an article in the Summer 1965 number of The University of Wales Review.